THE SEVEN DEADLY SINS

A Modern Day Interpretation of Humanity's Toxic Challenges with a Practical Spiritual Twist

KEVIN HUNTER

WARRIOR OF LIGHT PRESS

Los Angeles, California

Warrior of Light Press
www.kevin-hunter.com

Body, Mind & Spirit/Angels & Guides
Inspiration & Personal Growth

Acknowledgements

Thank you to Saint Nathaniel, my tough love guide in Heaven, as well as my Spirit team for your endless reservoir of support and guidance.

Chapters

Warrior of Light
mini-book pocket series

Spirit Guides and Angels
How I Communicate with Heaven

Soul Mates and Twin Flames
Attracting in Love, Friendships and the Human Heart

Divine Messages for Humanity
*Channeled Communication from the Other Side on Death, the
Afterlife, the Ego, Prejudices, Prayer and the Power of Love*

Raising Your Vibration
Fine Tune Your Body & Soul to Receive Messages from Heaven

Connecting with the Archangels

The Seven Deadly Sins
*A Modern Day Interpretation of Humanity's Toxic Challenges
with a Practical Spiritual Twist*

Author's Note

All *Warrior of Light* books are infused with practical messages and guidance that my Spirit team has taught and shared with me revolving around many different topics. The main goal is to fine tune your body, mind and soul. This improves humanity one person at a time. You are a Divine communicator and perfectly adjusted and capable of receiving messages from Heaven. This is for your benefit in order to live a happier, richer life. It is your individual responsibility to respect yourself and this planet while on your journey here.

The messages and information enclosed in this and all of the *Warrior of Light* books may be in my own words, but they do not come from me. They come from God, the Holy Spirit, my Spirit team of guides, angels and sometimes certain Archangels and Saints. I am merely the liaison or messenger in delivering and interpreting the intentions of what they wish to communicate. They love that I talk about them and share this stuff as it gets other people to work with them too!

There is one main hierarchy Saint who works with me leading the pack. His name is Nathaniel. He is often brutally truthful and forceful, as he does not mince words. There may be topics in this and my other books that might bother you or make you uncomfortable. He asks that you examine the underlying cause of this discomfort and come to terms with the fear attached. He cuts right to the heart of humanity without apology. I have learned quite a bit from him while adopting his ideology, which is Heaven's philosophy as a whole.

I am one with the Holy Spirit and have many Spirit Guides and Angels around me. As my connections to the other side grew to be daily over the course of my life, more of them joined in behind the others. I have often seen, sensed, heard and been privy to the dozens of magnificent lights that crowd around me on occasion.

If I use the word "He" when pertaining to God, this does not mean that I am advocating that he is a male. Simply replace the word, "He" with one you are comfortable using to identify God for you to be. This goes for any gender I use as examples. When I say, "spirit team", I am referring to a team of 'Guides and Angels'. The purpose of the *Warrior of Light* books is to empower and help you improve yourself, your life and humanity as a whole. It does not matter if you are a beginner or well versed in the subject matter. There may be something that reminds you of something you already know or something that you were unaware of. We all have much to share with one another, as we are all one in the end. This book and all of the *Warrior of Light* series of books contain information and directions on how to reach the place where you can be a fine tuned instrument to receive your own messages from your own Spirit team.

Some of my personal stories are infused and sprinkled in the books. This is in order for you to see how it works effectively for me. With some of my methods, I hope that you gain insight, knowledge or inspiration. It may prompt you to recall incidents where you were receiving heavenly messages in your own life. There are helpful ways that you can improve your existence and have a connection with Heaven throughout this book. Doing so will greatly transform yourself in all ways allowing you to attract wonderful circumstances at higher levels and live a happier more content life.

~ Kevin Hunter

THE SEVEN DEADLY SINS

Chapter One

THE SEVEN DEADLY SINS

The Seven Deadly Sins hail from a time when humankind believed that everything aside from breathing was a sin. There was a great deal of superstition born out of naivety. It was considered that if something or someone was offensive or unusual to what was culturally the norm, then it must be a sin. The intention here is to present the Seven Deadly Sins in a manner that the modern day world can relate to, comprehend, and connect with. Presenting it in a manner that applies today is effective than the fear based sins created during biblical ancient times. No one today is going to pay much attention to the outdated Seven Deadly Sins unless they're super religious, and even then you're not truly following it to the tee, but are adjusting it so that it applies to you personally. There are too many negative implications connected to the pre-dated Seven Deadly Sins.

Some have said that God hates those who exude the traits affiliated with the Seven Deadly Sins, but this is inaccurate. God does not hate, it is human ego that hates. The deadly sin traits are qualities not aligned with God, but the ego.

No one communicates in the archaic language that humankind used during biblical days. Members of my Spirit team use this language when they communicate with me, but I translate it in the current and modern language of my Earthly time so that others understand what is basically being said.

The Seven Deadly Sins have lost their meaning over the centuries. People have grown bored and disinterested in the sins because they feel it no longer applies to modern day life as they know it today. My Spirit team and I agreed it would be interesting to update the list with them in a way that is relatable to today's standards. There is a heavenly practical spiritual bent associated with it so that it is easier to grasp and identify with. This is not terribly unusual considering that many have updated the Seven Deadly Sins list to suit that specific time period.

The word *sin* is not in Heaven's vocabulary. We will continue to use it sporadically in order for you to understand the underlying message and intent. You are not going to Hell for abusing a sin, since the Hell that exists is the one you create within you. Hell is the one that humankind has created on Earth. The sins are not deadly, which is another dramatic word aligned best with the word *toxic*. The Seven Deadly Sins in today's language would be the Seven Toxic Challenges. This isn't to beautify the phrase, because both phrases mean the same thing.

Being aware of these toxic challenges are helpful because being in these states block or prevent one from achieving spiritual and practical greatness, finding peace in one's life, and picking up on the messages and guidance coming in from Heaven. The messages and guidance your Spirit team relays are intended to help guide you along the highest path. Heaven warns you of danger in your midst, or when you need to avoid something or someone that will bring harm to you. Your Spirit team can also nudge and guide you towards fulfilling work, relationships, and places to reside in that are suitable for your temperament.

The Seven Deadly Sins were traditionally designed in a way that no modern day soul can or will be able to follow, nor will they care. Various tests were run during the research stages of this book and targeted every type of person imaginable. This included those who identify to be deeply religious. It was discovered that every person on the planet would end up in some level of Hell for abusing a sin. Heaven will be a super deserted place if this were the case. The traditional Seven Deadly Sins are no longer realistic. It existed during a time when humankind was ultra superstitious, and yet the sins are traits your ego loves to abuse. There is a healthy and an unhealthy dark ego when it comes to the Seven Deadly Sins. We'll look at both the dark as well as the lights sides of the ego. Hate comes from the dark side of one's ego. If God is egoless, then the feeling of hate does not exist within Him. He is indifferent and not sitting back waiting to drop a house on someone for sinning. If that were the case, then there would be quite a bit of houses sitting on top of people by now.

The varying religions that exist on Earth were all adopted by the people in that particular culture. It was then taught and passed onto their offspring. That was until the offspring chose to break away from that and move into a more spiritual faith based belief system. On Earth, everyone has no choice, but to get along with one another regardless of your belief system. Whereas when you cross over to Heaven, you move into the areas with those who were like you and on the same spiritual path. If you were Buddhist, you move into the realms of those who were also practicing Buddhists. If you were Christian, you would move into the realms of those were practicing Christians on Earth and so forth.

In the end, all paths lead to God the one true source. No one religion has the market cornered on the subject and nor are they more special than anyone else.

In the Seven Deadly Sins, we will look at how Pride, Envy, Greed, Lust, Gluttony, Wrath, and Sloth are applied in today's world. This might seem like a serious subject, but we will keep it as basic, interesting and entertaining as possible.

After sifting through this book, you may discover how these challenges apply to the modern day world and in some areas of your own life.

Chapter Two

PRIDE

$\mathcal{E}$arthly life took a serious turn in the mid to late 1990's when usage of the World Wide Web and cell phones began to climb astronomically. Everyone was hopping on the industrial bandwagon, including ones Grandparents. Technological domination had gradually been rising over the century prior, but it blew up out of control post 1990's. By the time 2010 came around, the planet was the most populated its ever been and the use of some type of electronic device to connect with others became the norm.

Today, Earthly life is a world that functions primarily through technological devices, such as online, cell phones, and social media. Those from the Realm of the Star People are heavily responsible for bringing these great inventions to the world with the assistance of the Wise Ones. The positives to technology are endless, but so are the negatives. This technology boom also gave rise to the darkness of individual ego. As a result, narcissism commands human life and airing every shred of one's existence is pushed out into the open. Let's not forget the rule of the *selfie* flying out of control. A selfie is when you take a photo of yourself and then you send it out into the world by posting it on social media. Almost everyone has taken a photo of themselves with their cell phone. In my twenties, I was taking selfies with a digital camera long before social media and cell phones were the big thing. It had not blown up at that point yet. We were becoming curious humans wanting to have fun with these extraordinary devices. Somewhere along the way it moved past exploration and into obsession. This obsession turned into the noise that now plagues the universe.

Taking a selfie is not a crime, but in repetitive excess it often points to deeper issues or desires hidden within. If the mass majority is preoccupied with taking regular selfies, then what does that say about where Earthly life is at? I am the first to stand up and raise my hand and point out that I am guilty and conscious of abusing the selfie, but the key to any toxic challenge is being aware of it. It is being conscious of all that is around you, your behavior, and the actions you partake in. When looking into how you behave, you hold a mirror up to how you are and if that seems acceptable to you. Examine it deeply to get to the core of any personal issues that need to be addressed.

Human souls have a desire for love, respect,

and admiration. It is sought out from others in any way possible. This includes taking that good looking selfie and posting it online in order to receive that admiration and praise. What compels us to long and desire for positive compliments? Is the human race not getting it enough in our day to day life? Are we unfulfilled spiritually? One gentleman in a long term love relationship admitted to hanging out on phone dating/sex apps for the ego stroking. This includes posting different shirtless photos to see receive positive compliments from strangers, even though he assures that it doesn't go any further than that. He is loyal and monogamous to his love mate.

Everyone wants to connect and be loved. You dive down into your conscious to discover what needs to be addressed, or brings you to the realization in a manner that prompts you to be mindful of it. The ways to personally grow and evolve are by examining all that is around you and how it effects who you are. You grow and evolve when you make healthy positive changes in your life that can be seen to your higher self as another improvement for your souls sake while treading along your Earthly journey. Human life is all about trial and error. If you don't make positive changes, then you don't grow. You are intended to make mistakes and learn from them by cleaning up your act wherever necessary.

Many accuse others of being a narcissist, but at this point most anyone can be seen as narcissistic in today's world. Posting a selfie of you is an act of narcissism. It doesn't matter how innocent and harmless the selfie is. Narcissism and vanity have its extreme sides, where it's undisruptive to a point.

Others obsess over celebrities and how that celebrity's physical appearance looks, and the choices that artist makes in their personal life. The ego cannot wait to voice its disapproval. While both genders are targeted, it's women that receive higher amounts of criticism for some reason. They're also more prone to plastic surgery and other cosmetic enhancements in order to remain loved and admired. Human ego has equated age with something negative, when pre-technology days people respected those who were older. No one will be able to outrun age and this scares the planet. The current human life has been taught to view beauty in someone who is flawlessly perfect on the exterior. You have been taught to believe that you're something special because you're twenty-two and not sixty-two. When typically you are likely more evolved and experienced as you age, although this is not always the case. Some people will stay relatively where they are at any age.

Some of the things people say about celebrities photos are: "She doesn't look like she aged well at all." That's a kind sentence compared to some of the more negative stuff people dart into the universe online. The public will comment and argue with one another underneath the photo: "Let me introduce you to my new face." Or how about: "Did she get Botox!? She's perfect. I don't know why she would do that?"

Taking pride in oneself includes loving all that you are, what you do, or set out to do, pending it's not hurting anyone. Pride becomes dangerous when someone is intent on destroying another person because they live a different kind of a life than you do, or they prefer things that you do not. The dark side of pride is being arrogant, smug, or obsessed with vanity.

An example of vanity is the guy who constantly checks himself out in the mirror and toys with his hair and face. It is someone infatuated with their own exterior looks. They would be the person who desires relentless compliments from others about their exterior, even if their inner self falls flat. This temporarily inflates their sense of self, but like any toxic addiction, the craving for constant admiration never ceases. You base your worth on what others think or feel about you. When what others think about you should be irrelevant. What do you think about you? If you're unhappy with you, then what action steps can you take to correct that? Usually those obsessed with what others are doing, or how they appear are the ones who are spiritually dead and lacking in the positive inner self department.

It's challenging to escape the clutches of vanity since most everyone has taken selfies and posted them on their social media pages or phone chatting accounts at some point. Some do this act religiously by changing the photo almost daily for years. Discover where that fine line is drawn between having a healthy strong sense of love for yourself to crossing over into excessive narcissism.

One way that vanity becomes an issue is when someone who is super good looking and knows this fact well enough that they weave it in their social media or app profile: "Good looking girl here looking for the same." This is an example of a mixture of vanity, arrogant, smugness in top form. It is the dark side of pride basing ones existence on the exterior. The body is designed to age and fall apart. No human soul will ever be able to stop that from happening. You are a spirit temporarily inhabiting a human body for a specific purpose or purposes, and for a specific time period, then you will leave that rental known as your body. Avoid falling so far into vanity and physical appearance that you lose sight of who you are at the soul's core. You've spent your life obsessing over your looks and then you exit your body and are left with nothing to cling to.

Someone who is good looking and has a strong sense of inner self does not care about physical vanity to an extreme degree. They might know they're easy on the eyes, but it's not something of concern to them. They are humble when someone compliments them.

It might be surprising to know that not all good-looking people see themselves as attractive as others do. They admit to feeling lonely because others only pay attention to them because of how they look instead of who they are. This good-looking person is above superficiality, and intelligent on top of that. Because of this high intelligence quotient, they are interested in someone's good-natured character, personality, and heart, rather than if the person talking to them is good looking or not. When all you hear are physical compliments, it starts to move through one ear and out the other. It feels shallow and confusing to the intelligent good-looking person.

In the past, I would run tests with my photos to see how people would respond to them. I'd post a regular down to earth fully clothed shot and it wouldn't garner that much interest. I'd then post a shirtless sexy photo and suddenly everyone is going crazy and all over that like nobody's business. I would say, "It's the same person in both shots though, no? You liked me when I took my shirt off." It's no wonder everyone is posting sexy selfie shots. It's the only way anyone will pay any attention to them, yet more people admit to feeling disconnected and lonely in their life regardless.

Snapping that perfect selfie shot with your cell phone can be spontaneous or premeditated. Once you give the perfect face, whether you are pursing your lips, giving a sexy smirk, and showing just enough skin, then you snap the shot. You add filters or adjustments to the photo to give it a feeling as if a professional took the photograph. You upload it to your social media account where your followers click 'like' and comment with praises over how sexy or amazing you look. Do you feel validated in the end? Is the experience long lasting for you or is it a temporary high? How long before the high begins to wane? When it drops and you feel low again, do you prepare for another hot looking selfie? This is one sign where you know you have an addiction to vanity. I'm raising my hand here, because yes I have been guilty, but I'm aware of it in those cases.

Taking pride in your appearance is a positive

trait until it borders on vanity. Arrogant pride is when one thinks they're the bomb and better than everybody else. While this doesn't directly hurt or harm anyone, it can turn others off to you because you're displaying inflated self-importance that doesn't help in warming others up to you. It makes them feel small and less than, or it turns off the right people and brings in those you don't particularly want getting close to you. They are the shallow attracted in and drawn by your appearance or accomplishments. The question is, would they be able to stand you 24/7? What if we stripped away your good looks and accomplishments? You're still the same soul inside.

When everyone is performing in their higher self's space, then all are equal. Someone operating from their higher self is coming from a higher space than someone operating from their lower self. The higher self part of the soul doesn't need to be arrogant to get its point across. The higher self isn't concerned whether or not someone loves or appreciates them, because those qualities exist within them naturally. It is the lower self that will come off conceited in order to boost its accomplishments in someone's eyes for attention. The human ego desires love and admiration or it feels less than. Some will go to great lengths to have other human souls applaud and compliment them. This is a detachment from God, the light, the all knowing energy Creator. Excessive vanity and pride is a block that gets in the way of receiving heavenly messages and guidance.

There is a fine line one teeters when it comes

to any of the deadly sins or toxic challenges. When excessive pride turns into arrogance, then your energy grows moldy and dark.

Much of someone's life is governed online today. You will have your accomplishments listed on your website and social media accounts to promote yourself and your work. This is to give others a clue into who you are and what you've done with your life. It helps people get to know you and what business you're promoting. You have to do it to a degree if you're selling a product. You need to make money to survive and this is all part of the process. Everyone has gained a marketing degree when it comes to the promotion of oneself, even if you do not have a product to sell. Some have mastered this art of selling themselves. In a positive sense, this awakens ones creative spirit by finding clever ways to promote yourself.

The product that you're selling online is YOU. It's not who you truly are at your soul's core. It may be pieces of you. It might even be exaggerated or embellished since that is what marketing is in order to entice consumers. In this case, the consumer might be a potential date, friend, network connection, or love relationship. Those who are around you on a regular basis may not even know the real you. They will know you better than those on social media would know you. They know your facial expressions, your ticks, neurosis, and who you really are. When you're online you can be anybody you want to be. It gives one this ultra fascinating larger than life persona. You might come off extroverted on social media or apps, but then when someone meets you in person they discover you're quiet and keep to yourself. There is deception when communicating with anyone online. This is also why you want to guard your heart when you're conversing with someone new who you have not met in person yet. It can be dangerous to fall in love with someone you haven't met.

Arrogance, another form of pride, is when you attempt to dominate someone else by making sure they understand you are better than they are. It might be someone who says, "I'm better than you because I've got a college degree and you dropped out of High School." Having a college degree does not make someone a wonderful individual. The one who dropped out of High School may have gone onto accomplish greater circumstances, while the college graduate spends years struggling to find work. The one who dropped out of High School has humility and street smarts. Those are qualities that enhance your soul's growth. Having a college degree might make someone book smart, or help them get a particular job, but at the end of your life it is irrelevant unless you've developed soul enhancing qualities, which carry over into the next plane and other destinies.

The college graduate might feel small for not being able to find work in the field of their interest. It bothers their ego that the High School dropout runs a hugely successful business. Therefore, in order to boost their ego, they display the darker side of pride, which is arrogance in order to feel bigger than the High School dropout. Meanwhile, the High School dropout is the bigger individual because they're not attempting to dominate someone. They are satisfied with their personal accomplishments. They are proud of having dropped out of High School, but managed to start up a business that went onto become hugely successful. This High School dropout is observing the lighter side of pride.

Arrogant pride rules in the mind of the popular kid at school who puts down other people for not being what they perceive to be on their level. They have an exaggerated sense of self that is not based in reality. They believe they are awesome and better than everybody else simply because they're popular in grade school. This is the dark side of pride, while the lighter side is the unpopular kid who isn't concerned over who likes them. They are focused on building a life for themselves, rather than being loved during grade school. It is no surprise to find that in more cases than not, it is typically the unpopular kid in school who ends up being the success later in life. If you were or are that unpopular kid, know that you are destined for greatness!

Smugness is part of the arrogant pride family. Someone who is smug believes and knows how great they are even if others disagree. It doesn't matter if people love you or not as long as you love you. The smug person will go out of their way to ensure you understand how awesome they are. It's aligned with being too confident, but it is not as toxic as arrogance. Those operating from their lower self space are threatened by a confident person. It moves into dark smug territory when the individual goes out of their way to dominate others by pushing them down in order to boast about themselves. Someone who is better than someone else doesn't need to say it.

Having worked in the entertainment industry with well known talent, I learned that the bigger the star the nicer they are. I encountered lower level actors who are not well known or super well known that came off arrogant and smug. They expected others to bow down to them because it makes them feel as if they are a star. They will come off pushy and conceited in an attempt to bully others into bowing down to them. Bullies act out of fear. The ego fears it will not be respected, so it uses excessive force. Whereas the actual big stars, the A-list talent, and well known actors came off incredibly respectful, nice, compassionate, friendly, and giving. They did not need to hammer home how great they are, because they are in their higher self's space. They don't take what they've been handed to with disrespect. They are used to others fawning over them and did not grow a big head out of that, which would be the dark side of pride. Or perhaps on the way to the top they did have a large ego, but it was cut back down to size at some point through various scenarios. This gave them humility.

This is a generalization as there are stories out there of some difficult well-known stars being arrogant. In my personal work experience I never encountered a big star that was acting like that in my presence though. It was the unknowns who came off smug and arrogant. This is when you've moved into the dark side of pride. It is when you are bad-mannered and wanting others to immediately cater to your every whim.

The film business has quite a bit of people who operate from both the dark and light side of Pride. I've found the Producers mostly tend to be on the subdued introverted nice side, while the Agents came off boisterous, extroverted, and arrogant. This is another generalized stereotype of how it mostly is, even though there are some minimal exceptions here and there. The Producers I worked with and encountered took pride in their work, but they didn't come off vicious about it, which is moving into arrogance.

A one-time studio head chairperson at a major Hollywood studio landed in hot water when private work emails between her and a producer we're leaked online to the masses. It revealed them to be unpleasant people. The studio head resorted to derogatory name calling of some actors and implied racial slurs about the President of the United States at that time. She retaliated by admitting that the emails were insensitive, but were not a reflection of who she is. What you say and do is a reflection of you. It might not be how you are entirely, but it is a piece of who you are. In this example, she had a mirror placed in front of her to see that. What she saw was uncomfortable, so the natural reaction is to move into denial. "I'm not like that."

What is intended when issues like this pop up in your life is to be aware and conscious of how you are and have been behaving to date. Secrets can no longer be hidden and will be revealed at some point. This is the way it is in Heaven. Everything is laid out on the table for you to face and deal with, so that you can learn from it and enhance and grow your soul.

Admit to yourself that this is not a pleasant aspect of who you are, and then work on taking steps to change it and become a more compassionate person. Unfortunately, the studio head in this case never did admit to learning a lesson, but apologized along with the Producer. She said that if Hollywood we're nice that it wouldn't work. This is not true as I spent years inside Hollywood working with popular producers and talent. Every single person I worked with was compassionate, giving, and they still got the job done. They knew they didn't need to be a Neanderthal to get things done. In this case, the studio head operated from the dark side of pride never fully seeing the spotlight directed onto her by a hacker group.

These spotlights show up in your life when a wrong needs to be corrected. You can only get away with bad behavior and poor etiquette for so long before it catches up with you. The studio head and producer have had the reputation of being a megalomaniac, which is someone who has excessive pride about oneself. Assistants who have worked for them have horror stories that would make someone's stomach turn inside out. These are examples of those who are spiritually dead. They have decided they were victims instead of learning the lessons brought to them about their character. This is not uncommon when you live a life of excess. You become blinded by the physical glitter.

The work force is filled with egotistical human souls operating from a place of arrogant pride beyond this example. They believe this is the way to get things done, when in truth there are many compassionate successful executives who know how to get things done by treating everyone with equal respect and love.

While I will be the first to raise my hand once again that I have tons of pride, arrogance, and smugness, but I'm not cruel for the sake of being nasty to get something done. I still treat everyone with respect, until you are disrespectful.

The dark side of pride also comes in the form of holding a grudge against someone who you feel did not bow down to your needs. When someone approaches you to apologize for something, then you have smug arrogance about the apology. You might say, "They've got some nerve apologizing to me now after six months."

It is big of someone to issue a genuine apology for any wrongs they have caused you. At that moment, they have become the bigger person by reaching out to apologize for any ill will caused to you. By you offering humble forgiveness assists in wrapping up prior karma with that person. When you are unable to, then that is because your ego has expanded to the point where it is incapable of accepting it. That part of the karmic thread is complete when the person apologizes, and you genuinely offer forgiveness calling a truce. Both parties can be freed of the karmic thread and start a new life with a clean slate having accepted the lessons taught. Holding on to anger and unforgiveness festers and grows inside you. This blows up into health issues down the line, as well as blocks the flow of good stuff into your life.

The light side of pride is self confidence, self respect, and self worth. Having high self confidence is having a healthy self esteem. This is someone who is self assured and knows their value and worth. They don't come off as if they're being arrogant about it. They're not looking for praise when they accept the good they've accomplished. It is someone who goes at it alone, or against the crowd because it's something they believe in. Even when others mock, criticize, or judge them, they still do what they believe in and ignore the naysayers. This is someone with a healthy sense of pride and confidence. It inspires and empowers others instead of turning them off. Someone with self-confidence leads by example.

People see the self confident person and admire them, because that person isn't putting anyone down. They're not doing things in order to impress others, or to get someone's attention, which is the dark side of pride. The light side is doing things that matter to you regardless if you're liked or not.

When someone admires the self confident person then the confident person says, "Thank you. I appreciate that."

Whereas the opposite is someone blowing off the one who has paid you a compliment. This is someone arrogant and over confident. That person instead smugly says, "Thanks. I already know how great I am."

The self confident person works hard and enjoys what they do. They do not require positive praise from a superior, their employer, peers, or the public. Reaching a healthy sense of self confidence means loving who you are without desiring any attention about it. Look back on your accomplishments and strengths and be proud of that.

Self-worth is also having a healthy self esteem that includes knowing your worth and understanding how loved you are by Heaven. When you do not have a high self esteem, then this can cause you to become perpetually depressed and unmotivated. The opposite extreme is having exaggerated narcissistic tendencies about one self.

When someone has low self worth, they are prone to become addicted to toxins such as drugs, alcohol, or food. They will get into poisonous relationship connections out of loneliness, or because they do not think highly of themselves enough to escape a toxic connection. They might be lucky enough to get into a relationship with someone who is good for them, but then they will sabotage it because they do not feel they are worthy of a great love connection.

The person with low self worth might say, "This feels too good to be true and I cannot believe something this great is happening for me. I'm going to end it since I will ruin it eventually anyway." Or they will feel the person is too good for them and therefore will disrupt it at some point in the end.

Having a high sense of self worth is to love all that you are. You're aware you have flaws, but you don't really care. This is who you are and you love every bit of it. If it's a toxic flaw, then you work on that privately.

Some have a general great sense of self worth, but then they log online and see some hot popular guy or girl and the negative self talk starts to creep up. "I wish I looked that good. They're so lucky they look like that and I only look like this."

You end up experiencing a teeter-totter effect where one day you're on cloud nine and know your worth. That is until you read or see something online that kicks you down. Luckily, this type of person bounces back easily, but there are others who move through life always feeling a low sense of self worth. Love all that you are and be proud of that. You are loved by God and your Spirit team around the clock no matter what. You are important and much needed at this time in history. Don't fall into the ego's trap that you are not worthy.

The lack of solid long-term love relationships has caused others to feel low self worth. Someone leaves you abruptly and you wonder if there is something wrong with you. You go down the list, "Maybe it was that I gained weight, or that I'm not attractive to them anymore. Or maybe it was that I was too boring, not exciting enough, or not emotionally available."

Your mind sifts down the endless lists of possibilities as to why your lover left you. It crushes your self-esteem and hurts your pride until you begin empowering exercises that lift your vibration into loving all that you are. When someone leaves you, it doesn't matter how great you look or how wonderfully giving you are. They have varying reasons for leaving you that likely do not have anything to do with you.

Feeling good about all that you are increases your self-worth. Exercise lifts me into optimism and gives me a boost of energy when I'm floundering, tired, or moody. Suddenly I'm on cloud nine after biking or going for a jog.

Self-respect means value all levels of yourself from the soul, mind, and body. You know you've made mistakes at times and you've owned up to them. You have dignity and integrity. You're honest in your dealings with others. You take pride in all that you are and your accomplishments. You don't do things or get involved with others that do not feel right to you.

Having self respect means you speak highly of yourself, but it's not to the point of overkill. The traits associated with pride are about walking that fine line between loving yourself, but not to the point of full on narcissism. Narcissism is when it's all about you and you do not care about others in any measure of ways.

Everyone exudes both the dark and light sides of pride, but these are more about the offenders who operate purely in the space of the dark side of it. It's someone who is arrogant, smug, or vain full time. It's natural to slip once in awhile from having self confidence, and then having it increase into arrogance. Generally someone who is good natured at heart is not residing in the dark side of pride to begin with. They respect themselves and those around them, pending others are giving them this equal respect too.

Chapter Three

ENVY

$\mathscr{Y}$ou witness someone else's success, good looks, or any other positive attributes about them, then the pessimistic feelings rise up within you causing you to feel envious. Envy is when you experience negative emotions over what someone else has that you don't. It's moving into a space of lack. You grow depressed because you've allowed who they are, what they look like, or what they have to convince you that they're better than you. They have what you perceive to be "gifts".

Envy leads one to become angry or resentful because you feel more superior than this other person. You have a difficult time understanding why wonderful things are happening for them and not you. You feel as if you are better than they are and more deserving of the success or good looks they seem to be blessed with.

There isn't a soul on the planet that doesn't have at least one gift. Everyone has something special about them even if you feel that is not the case with you. You came into this life with these gifts in order to utilize it to your advantage while here. This means applying the gifts into your life purpose and dealings with others. No one has the same gifts as everybody else. Avoid becoming blindsided over what you feel a gift is. Good looks are not a gift or a blessing, because the physical appearance will fade in every single human being roaming the planet. Who you are inside and what you set out to do is a gift. Having love and compassion for all is a gift. Look at the things you enjoy doing that are not hurting someone else and connect that to a gift you've been bestowed with. What you do with that gift is up to you.

You grow envious when you see someone who has what you believe to be the perfect physical appearance, and you become depressed or angry over it. Depression symptoms rise due to this insecure feeling of low self worth. You believe you don't look as good as this other person. In the process, you give this other person power over you. The media perpetuates sexy eye candy images in front of the public daily. This will take its toll on others who see these images causing them to become resentful. It is not a healthy fixation as it tampers with your self esteem. The most gorgeous appearing person is not seen as attractive to everyone on the entire planet. Not everyone is attracted to the same type of person.

There are factors associated with good looks or

a nice physical appearance. Some people are physically attractive in your eyes due to human genetics, or by taking care of themselves regularly through diet, nutrition, beauty upkeep, and exercise. The images put out there in the media are altered digitally, carefully designed, and airbrushed to the extreme making the person appear especially beautiful and unreal. Besides everyone looks great back home on the other side.

I've worked with and hung out with many well known people in the entertainment industry. They appear like anybody else behind closed doors. Often times they are dressed down and without make-up that many might not even recognize them. When it's time for them to get in front of the camera, they disappear into a make-up, hair, and wardrobe trailer only to emerge appearing out of this world where jaws are dropping. They suddenly look like that movie star everyone is accustomed to knowing. This is because there is a team of paid people helping them get camera ready. Add to that the great lighting and hi-tech cameras being used, it's no wonder this has falsely deceived the world into believing these people roll out of bed looking like this. Today the average user can easily touch up their photos and selfies, which give the illusion of being a model. It gives one a false impression or delusion of who you think they are. No one looks that incredible every second of their life.

Exterior beauty fades rather quickly. Even the most great looking person has a good ten years of physically appearing that way before signs of aging begin to take place. You might have youthful good looks for about twenty years, from say aged fifteen to thirty-five, but then your physical exterior looks gradually decline. For others, it may even be a good ten years and the decline starts. This is part of the nature of the human physical body, since you are renting your body for a limited time to live an Earthly life for more important purposes than looking like a model.

One of the many recurring messages those in Heaven pass onto human souls is to take care of yourself. This means taking care of you and the body and life you've been given as best you can. This isn't for the reasons of vanity, but because they know that when you take care of yourself inside and out, then you have more energy to accomplish what you set out to do. You have a lower risk of attracting in negative health issues that can hit you at some point in your life. It raises your vibration, which lifts you into positive feelings of joy, love, and peace. You have a stronger self confidence and feel good about yourself.

You're not intended to obsess over age and physical looks to the point where it is permanently embedded in your psyche. Those who are discriminatory over someone's looks or age are the ones who are hit hardest with it when they grow older. They are discriminatory or ageist because they have low self esteem. There is something they're unhappy with about themselves. When the ego is miserable it will attack others in order to give itself a boost. It's perception is not based in reality. Someone with strong self esteem is not attacking others, but praising them and saying,

"Good for you!"

Ageism is an obsessive craze in current human life. Popular culture has trained the masses to view aging as something negative. Senior citizens receive the brunt of prejudices surrounding age. As I grew older, the comments I receive from others soon became, "You look great for your age!" While it is seemingly a compliment as if one is impressed, it is not an accomplishment to applaud oneself for. The irony about those who are ageist is that if they live a full life, they too will be a senior citizen at the last part of their life run.

The ageist is building up Karma through this discrimination. The Karma will be paid back in varying ways such as causing them to suffer as they age. It will be something they do unto themselves realizing that the ageing thing is now happening to them. This isn't a form of punishment, but to teach the soul humility. They get to live in the shoes of the ones they were once criticizing. You cannot control your age. It also has no relevance in the grand reality, because once you pass on back home, your age is irrelevant. Some souls living an Earthly life are hundreds of years old. They have had many repeated lives for various reasons. Some of that might be to balance out past Karma, for the purpose of being a teacher, or other reasons that benefit that soul or humanity. Every year you spend on Earth is another year older in human years. When you cross over back home, you're brought back to the highest most incredible state possible, both inside and out. You no longer care, because the Earthly physical limitations are stripped away from you. The heavy burdens have dissolved and you're in a perfect state of bliss and contentment. What matters is your integrity, and who you are deep down at your soul's core. What's important is what you set out to do with your life that benefits humanity in a positive way. Why is the darkness of ego obsessed about over shadowing someone's accomplishments by bringing up someone's age, gender, race, or sexual orientation? One hopes that humanity will continue to progress as a society to where you no longer keep track of those insignificant details.

Taking care of your physical body is vital for your health, overall well being, and state of mind. It is also to help you become a fine tuned up machine with a crystal clear communication line with Heaven.

Those who become envious over someone else will sulk and pout inside. They might retaliate in the form of an attack against someone who has great things happening for them. This is seen in comments all over the Internet. Comments are unhealthy to read as it lowers your vibration and keeps it there until the work is done to re-raise it. There is a celebrity story posted by the media and the darkness of ego in humankind chooses to post an attack about that celebrity. They'll attack the celebrity's looks or talent through venomous graphic words. This is a form of envy because someone who is not envious of someone is not operating from the space of hate. All forms of attack come from the ego. Someone who uses less dark ego is indifferent to anything that could potentially cause them to react negatively.

Envy is also a wasted emotion and stems from two different forms of feeling. One is from a sense of low self worth that you're not good enough or important. The other is anger and resentment that someone appears to have all the luck. Feel good about yourself no matter what. Feel good about all that you are - flaws and all. Avoid wasting time on being envious. Do not allow someone else's accomplishments, traits, or looks, to bring you down as if you're not worthy. You are worthy!

Perhaps you're a hard worker who excels at your job and yet you're living paycheck to paycheck. You work harder than any other around you. You see the gifts of abundance being bestowed upon someone else who you feel is less than you. This is your ego being extra sure of itself to the point where you feel envy. You'll want to move that envy into something positive that can work to your benefit. Feeling down or resentful because someone receives great things will not help you in attracting in what you desire. Negative feelings have low vibration energy within it. This is what attracts downbeat circumstances into your world. It is a block that prevents the positive flow of abundance into your life. The person you're envious of is not concerned in the slightest with what they have or what others have. They're just doing their work and believing in it. This is what contributes to the abundance being handed to them.

When deep envy is present, then it can drive one into malice. Malice is when you become offended by someone else to the point that you're pushed to inflict harm on that person. This is witnessed with the behavior of bullies who harass or target others because there is something about them they are secretly envious of. They cannot comprehend or relate to anyone who is different than them. Malice and bullying comes from a basic primal instinct reaction to something that is not understood. In that state, your lower self and ego rule your life. The soul's ego has not raised into a higher consciousness where one is able to embrace all parts of life. It is functioning in a limited way unable to broaden one's mind to see that not everyone is the same. There are no clones on Earth. Most everything primal is inherited and taught to you by your surroundings. If you're a world traveler, then you've visited other countries, states, or towns, and then witnessed how everyone residing in that particular area is similar to one another. Sometimes you visit a foreign country and notice how the culture is vastly different from yours. You're accepting of it because you're open to understanding all walks of life as a world traveler.

The envious bully is incapable of relating to someone who is different from them. There is the statement that says in order to understand another person, you need to walk in their shoes. This is experiencing what they perceive to be their reality even if you morally disagree with it. Gifted actors are especially able to accomplish this. They can take the most difficult hateful character and find the heart of that person. This is because even the most hateful person has a heart of gold, even if it's buried underneath life circumstances and dark ego. The angels see who that soul is even if that soul has forgotten.

There are times where every soul on the planet has committed the crime of envy. Sometimes it is done unintentionally without realizing you've reacted in an inappropriate way over what someone said or did. Where it turns into malice is when you retaliate with the intent to harm. Malice comes from the Latin words *evil* or *bad*.

The ego is a powerful force within you that quickly turns dark unleashing a hellish monster. When it feels bruised by what someone said, it will strike back using malicious force to make sure you understand it's in charge. It does not like to be dominated and will react in a dangerous tantrum. No one should endure or tolerate disrespect and abuse of any kind on any level. Sometimes you are placed in a position where you have to defend yourself against harsh words darted at you out of nowhere. The fine line is how you choose to retaliate. Do you move into nasty envious malice? Or do you use assertive language when explaining to the offender that the words they've used on you is inappropriate? It's greatly efficient to be diplomatic and speak assertively when talking to someone who has crossed your boundaries. Assertiveness is true inner spirit power at the helms. If the words do nothing to influence the bully, then walk away. Taking the high road is walking away and ignoring it. If you operate from a space of being as egoless as possible, then you're unaffected or jarred by harsh words darted at you.

Call on the Archangel Michael to shield you with protective white light. This is in order to keep all of that toxicity out. If someone enters this sphere, ask Archangel Michael to remove them immediately.

Prejudice is another negative result of envy. Humankind in general is territorial of its surroundings and can be undoubtedly led by those around them. If someone moves into their environment that is different from the rest of that community, then disdain and prejudice is formed. This prejudice can move into malice when you react to what you disapprove of in violent ways, such as harassing that individual. Constant bullying, harassing, and violence is seen in great numbers around the world and all throughout history. People feel disgust or envy towards others who are not like them. The darkness of one's ego feels it is superior to all others instead of equal and on the same playing field.

Prejudice is one of the great traits connected to the downfall of humanity. It causes unnecessary anger, resentment, envy, and hate in humankind. If someone is not white, heterosexual, and rich, then disdain is experienced. Yet, by stating that line, it in itself is prejudicial against the white, heterosexual, rich. There is prejudice against all races, as well as the rich and the poor. Prejudice exists against the old, the young, the handicap, the fit, the unfit, the successful, and the unproductive. It's present against all religions, gender, sexual orientations, and political affiliations. The underlying trait that has propelled wars, fighting, crime, and power, is due to some form of envy and prejudice.

Viewing human beings and the lives they created from a higher perspective gives one a broader slant. Human beings are viewed as ants gnawing and clawing at one another in absurdity.

Prejudice is a characteristic that turns into malice and bullying when triggered. Everyone is harassing each other, and tolerance or constructive words to bridge extreme parties together are thrown out the window.

The one common reason all are here is to love, but extreme sides of the darkness of one's ego refuse to meet in the middle in order to begin the process of achieving that space. These differences are choices one makes through the developmental stages of how you were raised. You were not born this way. There are many cases where human souls do evolve out of hatred. These stories are also brought to light publicly where a well known figure admits to evolving or changing their stance on something they once loathed. Stand dangerously close to the middle even if you stand alone. The brave and the centered find this space naturally from within. You are seeing others through the eyes of the angels when you view circumstances out of the lenses of another.

The opposite of envy is to admire. Instead of

feeling envy over someone else's achievements, the less than counterproductive feeling is to admire them for what they've accomplished. It empowers you and lifts you up to go after what you desire. It should remind you that anything is possible and everyone has positive gifts to contribute to the world.

All words have positive or negative vibration energy in it. When one vocally admires another it sounds pleasant than someone vocally expressing disdain. Envy is a lower energy vibration feeling and word. It does nothing to help you or anyone. The word *admire* has a positive vibration energy to it. The action of admiring another causes no pain nor does it have any harmful connotations to it. However, having too much admiration can turn the energy of the word into something toxic. Admiration can be taken to the extreme and turn into obsession. Obsession can be when you compulsively think about someone or something to the point where a block has been created in your life. You check the social media page of someone you're romantically interested in daily to see what they're up to. This can be worse when it's an ex, because you have not been able to let go of that person who seems to have moved on by the posts you read from them.

A parent has huge admiration for their child to the point where the child learns to take advantage of that. The child expects automatic admiration from others because it grew up getting away with murder so to speak. The child learns to lie, manipulate, and deceive. This is carried over into their adult life. They're the ones that have the frequent tantrums as an adult to get others to bow down to their every whim. The flipside is a child who was ignored growing up. They could grow up to demand attention from others because it was something that was missing in adolescence. All souls desire love and companionship on some level. The basic physical human condition is much like animals roaming in packs. There is always a leader in these packs. This is the guy or girl who toots his own horn and doesn't follow the herd. The one not following the herd is the leader, even if others have not yet taken the bait at the time of that person's life. This is especially the case with a child or teenager who moves in another direction than their peers.

When you have admiring pride for oneself, then that gives one a healthy self esteem. You admire and appreciate who you are and know how to take care of all aspects of you. When you are taken care of, then it is a natural act to move it into taking care of others, whether this is in your work life, or in your love relationships.

If you are in a relationship, then admire yourself as much as you appreciate your partner. This makes for a happy healthy connection. If one has admiration for their love partner, but the other partner secretly has envy for you, then this taints the connection. It becomes a lopsided, unbalanced, and unrequited love. The toxins from the envious partner seep into the love relationship causing it to bleed in from the edges.

The act of *loving* is the opposite of envy. This

means be loving towards yourself or another. There is a high vibration energy darted outwardly into the Universe and returned back to you when you display loving traits. Healthy long term loving relationships tend to show the partners as happy and healthier than those who are not in those types of connections. This is not saying that those who choose to be single are miserable, but being in a loving soul mate partnership connection tends to enhance one another. This is where neither partner is envious of the other in this relationship. Instead they build each other up naturally with support, love, and admiration. There is nothing one cannot accomplish while in a strong love connection with someone. It motivates and inspires you to carry on in life in the right spirit.

Love connections that lack in mutual admiration begin to crumble bit by bit as time progresses on. In this case, one is better off single and happy, rather than in a relationship and miserable.

It's the human condition to desire love, admiration, and companionship to an extent. There is no cure all in relationships, but human souls become satisfied by being in a love connection where there is a mutual respectful companionship. When one partner begins to lose interest and moves away emotionally from loving their partner to becoming envious, then the toxins seep into the partnership eroding it from the inside out until it's fully destroyed.

When one experiences loving and admiring feelings, then this raises your vibration and empowers you. Empowerment is having inner strength and confidence in all that you are and what you set out to do. It is being courageous and lovingly bold. There is nothing you cannot do when you are empowered. Where the dark side of envy destroys, the light side lifts one up into a magical place. Empowering oneself is all part of loving and admiring all that you and others are. You might notice you have flaws you fixate on. If this is the case, then you take action steps to change that if it's possible, or you accept and love it. Taking action to improve something is empowering oneself.

Chapter Four

GREED

Your needs and desires can take over and build morphing into greed. Everyone longs for something in their life, whether it's material, physical, or spiritual based substances. The act of longing for something or someone is not as toxic as the nature of greed. Greed causes the darkness of ego to perform despicable acts in order to gain what it desires. Whereas the act of longing is an obsessive empty feeling inside developed by a voracious need to obtain something you do not have.

Black Friday takes place the day after the United States celebrated holiday *Thanksgiving*. It is considered one of the busiest shopping days of the year. It is also a day you want to steer clear of heading into retail outlets or braving the streets.

You're aware of this if you have a higher degree of psychic input and sensitivity. You know what kind of energies will harshly tamper on your system. You sense every nuance and know to avoid going to a mall or promenade on most days let alone Black Friday.

The word and color *Black* in *Friday* has held up to its name since it truly is a dark day. You will bear witness to the violent atrocities and malicious actions and behaviors that come out of others who will do anything to retrieve a material item that is heavily discounted. The greed energy prevails the ego and rules the planet more than it ever has to date. If something is offered for free, or at a huge discount, then the masses go trampling over each other to get it. This is an example of greed making it one of the seven deadly sins and toxic challenges in human kind.

Material and shopping are some of the areas that greed dominates and reveals its ugly devil horns. Everywhere you turn there is a sale, or a company is advertising their products in a variety of ways to lure consumers into it. Businesses need to make money in order to thrive and survive. They will offer sales and advertise as a way to get their products in front of you. This is not a problem until it invites in famished human souls hungry enough to knock one another down to get to it.

Resembling all of the deadly sins, there are good and bad aspects to greed. There is nothing wicked with wanting the latest phone that was released, until it pushes you to act in heinous ways to get it. Standing in line the day a product is released is due to an uncontrollable anxious feeling where you must have this or you will die. It's not hurting anyone because you race to the store super early pumped up with excitement to get that phone the day it's released. Does it make a difference if you take your time getting it? The phone is not going anywhere and will still be available a week or two after it's released. It's also less risky to wait it out. If there is a nationwide technological problem with the product, then the company that made it can issue an update on the phone to correct that before you make that big purchase.

Greed becomes dangerous when you push, shove, harm, and walk all over others to get what you desire. The ego feels there isn't enough to go around. It will convince you that you must have that toy before anyone else gets their hands on it. It is the ego attempting to dominate and feel in control and powerful at all costs.

Type into your Internet search browser the phrase: *Black Friday Greed*. You will find endless pages of how this nasty toxic greed behavior governs others lives. There are countless reports and videos of crimes being filmed on that day. It displays the harm that others commit on one another out of greed. People trample over each other like cattle. They knock others down viciously resulting in bodily harm and in some cases death. Many camp out all night long to buy things at a discount, while others verbally assault anyone around them for taking the last product on the shelf. Some resort to physical violence on others.

The companies that are open for business only

care about making money. They know it could be a big financial gain, therefore they have no intention of shutting down for the day. This greed mentality and harm is over money and material possessions, which becomes obsolete and non-existent the second you leave your body and this plane. Money is the only God that the greedy worship rendering themselves soulless.

In order to survive on this planet, money is needed. You need money for clothes, food, transportation, housing, and hopefully a little extra left over for personal luxuries. Money is a problem when it drowns the spirit. This lack mentality blocks the flow of abundance in your life.

Violent crimes are birthed out of a longing, excessive, greed. In non-peaceful protests, human souls burn their own neighborhoods down to the ground. This is out of anger over something that has happened in the media. In the end, they are left with far less than they had to begin with. Anything other than peaceful protesting does nothing to help anyone. The dark ego prompts others to destroy anything in its wake from property to people. How many cases have you heard where violent protests have worked and brought upon a positive solution?

Excess is when you long to obtain more than you need. God will assist those who help themselves. This is to help with obtaining what is beneficial to you and not necessarily what you want. Some of the super rich are guilty of excess by purchasing more than they need. While having tons of money is not a sin, it is when you become enslaved to it.

I witnessed my father in this lifetime break his back working like a dog to make money for things that were ultimately taken away from him upon his deathbed. He wasted his life misguided by greed and naivety. Although he instilled in me a strong work ethic, I luckily did not fall down the path of greed, as I have no desire for anything that does not contribute to living comfortably enough without worry as all do on some level.

Driving a big SUV car can be living beyond your means and in the realm of excess. The debatable exception is if the person is using the extra space for lugging huge items or trucking many kids around on a regular basis. People have had many children in the past long before SUV's existed. They managed to function without driving extra large cars they are unable to maneuver. Not to mention the high amounts of toxins and pollutants being emitted into the air. This contributes to the disintegration of this beautiful planet.

Greed and excess contributes to waste. Waste is toxic trash piled sky high of unnecessary valuables one has placed great emphasis on to be important or of worth. Your soul is valuable, but that broken trinket you refuse to throw away is likely not. After a death of someone near you, one of the steps is to dissolve their assets and clean up. When my father passed away, we discovered everything in shambles with waste piled all over the place. He was a hoarder, which comes from a greed, excess, and lack mentality. You do not need to save every shred of trash imaginable. This contributes to blocking the flow of natural positive energy in your life. It's chaotic energy that perpetuates the flow of good abundance attempting to get in. This is why some hire a decorator, Zen artist, or Feng Shui expert to help set up their homes in a way that allows for a positive flow of energy through their environment.

Greed plays a major role in the lives of humanity. Notice how consumers treat sales people or how diners treat servers. Greed causes others to file a lawsuit or complaint over the slightest triviality. Once in awhile, it is reversed where a sales person or someone in a store or organization is rude or hostile to a consumer for no reason at all. Have an understanding of what that person might have gone through before you arrived. Maybe they had a dramatic situation happen to them in their personal life that day, or they dealt with a customer who ruined their day by giving them a hard time just before you walked in. Having strong empathy is by putting yourself in someone else's shoes without judgment.

This is about the mantra that says, *"The customer is always right."* It was created during a time when the customer was typically right. It was before humanity expanded into greed.

Longing is a lower form of greed, but it doesn't have the abusive energy associated with it that greed has. There are underlying toxins within and around it. Longing for something you do not have causes pain, sadness, and frustration. None of this energy helps in attracting what you desire. Instead it causes further grief harming aspects of your life at some point.

Everyone longs for something from time to time. It's a natural human experience to long for the basic necessities of life such as a love relationship, a home, or a good career. Where it becomes a problem is when your thoughts feel this strong longing for something specific daily for months and even years. When these longing feelings have been prolonged it can manifest into greed where you will stop at no cost to obtain what you want. Work on adjusting your thoughts and feelings to that of optimism. Pray, ask for help, take action, and let the positive energy flow into you. What action steps can you take to bring what you desire to you quicker?

Self-Control is the opposite of greed. Having self control is when you utilize restraint from impulsive reckless urges that can wreak havoc on you or another person. Some souls have an easier time at using self control. They might be super disciplined when it comes to their emotions or feelings, while someone else might be triggered to a higher level of upset immediately upon hearing something that troubles their ego.

There are varying degrees of emotional reactions that are delivered by the ego. Someone who doesn't fly off the handle and uses self control is able to take their time in making sound decisions that benefit themselves or someone else. They make great executives, leaders, or someone in charge.

Using self control where emotions are concerned prevents the dark part of your ego from reacting immediately without thinking. When it makes decisions irrationally, then this will cause harm or issues to your life or another. Someone who takes their time assessing a situation after having absorbed upsetting information is able to tune into their Spirit team in assisting with the formation of an adequate or diplomatic response or action.

Using quite a bit self control over the course of my own life has prompted others to point out often that my emotions seem to be on an even keel. Some have used the phrase, "The calm within the storm." This is how it appears on the outside, but on the inside is where this turbulent storm is taking place. Wise Ones have that darkness hanging pretty close to the surface. Known for their tempers when any form of disrespect is shown. Two of the reasons I'm here is to teach about love and respect, so it's no surprise that when neither are exuded that it can unleash this anger. Otherwise, there is that consistent stable calm love moving through me.

The self-control my team is talking about here is applied to those who live for drama. Every other response out of this drama filled person is emotionally driven to create chaos in their lives or the lives in others. This is seen with gossip columnists and the media who use dramatic words to titillate the public in forming a lynch mob against another. This is an example of having no self control.

Emotional levels are not the only aspects affected by not having self control. When you have self control, then you're not attracted to an excess of anything. You are able to use restraint and commanding reign over your ego. You make decisions methodically instead of through reckless impulses to go after anything that is toxic. Unable to go a day without having an alcoholic drink is tied to not having self control, but it is also a human inherited genetic gene.

One of my many toxic addictions was to alcohol. I could drink anyone under the table when I was in my early twenties. Now I can go for weeks and even months and not crave a drink. I understand what it's like to be addicted, since I'm one of the biggest addicts of all.

You might have total self control when it comes to your emotions, but the greed can creep up in other areas in your life.

The dating world today primarily lives on social media and mobile phone apps. This has also contributed to the ego moving swiftly into the space of greed. You message dozens of people each day with an aloof detachment only to discard them one by one and start all over again the next day. You're not grasping the concept that there is a person behind that profile photo. The person is seen as an object when you have aloof emotion to them. With all the choices of people to chat with daily, it has led to greed instead of using self control and being selective over who you will work on developing a connection with. This partially adds to why so many complain to be perpetually single and lonely. They're unable to build lasting connections with anyone, because their focus veers onto someone new days later searching for the perfect unflawed person that doesn't exist.

Self control is doing things in moderation. Moderation is a healthy balanced level of doing something that can be perceived as toxic where you only do it once in awhile and in low quantities. It's something you could go for weeks without if you wanted to. Someone has a love for drinking wine, but they do it in moderation. Instead of drinking a bottle of wine a night, they're drinking a glass or two every few days.

Humankind moves through their individual stressful lives all around the world. There is too much burden to carry on your back day after day. You desire meaning, comfort, and security. You reach for relief in any way you can, even if it's in the form of a toxin. Whether it's from drugs, alcohol, pills, food, sex, or any other means. Refraining from anything toxic in high abundance is always advised, but if that's been a struggle for you, then work on reducing it to moderation, where it's only once in awhile or in low quantities. This was how I gradually reduced or dissolved many of the toxic substances I had immense greedy attraction for. I knew it couldn't be good for me and wanted to stop or slow down. With the help from Heaven, I would do the toxin less and less over time. It was a gradual reduction of the toxin until I realized months had gone by and I was no longer using or abusing it.

One trait that successful people have is self discipline. They know how to use restraint when it comes to doing things that could potentially cause their downfall. They are hardworking, persistent, and passionate about what they set out to do. Nothing will stand in their way of that. Others will scoff at someone's self disciplined attitude. They will criticize them as being too rigid, but this is why the self disciplined person is successful and the one scoffing about it is not. This self-discipline carries beyond career or work related endeavors and into other areas of your life. This includes relationships, your life force, spiritual pursuits, and overall health and well-being. When you lack self discipline, then you head down paths that are rocky and full of thorns. You fall into destructive patterns by consuming toxic vices, which not only delay any kind of success, but block divine guidance that helps you along your higher self's path.

Chapter Five

LUST

When one considers the meaning of *lust*, it is automatically connected to sex. The traditional perception of lust as a deadly sin will say there isn't anything wrong with having sexual desire since God created sexual desire in order to keep the human race going. This can no longer be used as an argument or fact since my team points out that there are seven billion people on the planet at this time in history. Rest assured there will never be any threat of the human race coming to a halt because everyone has stopped fornicating. The human race was able to multiply with no problem from just two people on the planet at the beginning of humankind, so you may wipe away any fear surrounding the death of the human race from your mind.

Human beings have expanded in population to the point where people are spilling off the edges of the planet. If a decade went by and no baby was born during that time, it would not hurt procreation. The overload humankind created has wreaked havoc on Earthly existence. This has caused humankind to claw, fight, and scream for attention. Jobs are no longer plentiful since there are more people than there are work. The rest of the working world sits in their cars in sandwiched in traffic day after day disconnected from anything outside of physical distractions. This one tiny act alone places heavy stress on someone's back that increases the opportunities for greater health risks that would not exist if the planet were not so plentiful with people. This is debunking the mythology that states God intended you to multiply. This was understood when there were only two people on the planet.

Someone does not need to be told to multiply. Human ego has no problem figuring out that when a male connects sexually with a female that the result is a child. This is the case all across the animal kingdom. Animals didn't need to be told or taught to multiply. They do it on their own as it's part of their innate nature.

Lust is part of the deadly sin list because of the issues that are born out of it when used and abused to excess. My whole aura has screamed sex since adolescence, therefore I have a personal understanding of the infinite struggles that exist surrounding lust. A healthy sexual appetite is not to be confused with drowning in lust. The act of lust is a craving for something you do not have, or have not experienced, but greatly yearn for. This is whether it is sexual in nature, or a desire for an object with intense blinding passion. It is a deep thirst that can lead to something toxic when it is what primarily drives you.

Lust from a sexual perspective can lead to pornography addiction. Pornography was taught over the centuries to be viewed as negative, because anything sex related scares some of humankind. However, like any deadly sin there is a fine line between when it crosses over to toxic challenge territory.

Pornography addiction can be abused where it consumes you every second of every day. Not only does it prevent you from getting to work on life related matters, but it can hurt and strain your connections. When consumed by pornographic images on a regular basis, then this raises the bar as to how you believe a man or woman should look. Pornographic images are not always nude related. They can be the hyper sexualized images that the media and popular culture put in front of human souls on a regular basis. When this is all you see every time you're online, then it becomes blinding in the sense that it prevents you from viewing Earthly life in a clearer way beyond the physical. Pornography addiction gives one a false view of how one must perform in bed. You discover this is unrealistic when you connect with another physical being who is unable to measure up to your built up fantasy. As a result, you would rather be alone and view porn to reach a higher sexual state, than connect with someone.

There are many singles who have never been in a

love relationship, let alone on a proper date. They have never had any luck connecting and meeting with someone with the idea of eventually having sex. Instead they spend their days growing lonely, disconnected from others, and feeling unloved. Perhaps they're not physically attractive to anyone that has come across them. Or they have other issues which prevent them from being able to connect with someone in a love or sexual connection. This is where pornography use can be seen as a lifesaver to that person. There are a great deal of human souls who desire affection, love, and attention. When all of that is lacking and there is a disconnect from the Divine, then this gives rise to you going on a search to find this love in any area possible.

There are those who are attractive or considered a catch to others, yet they have tremendous social anxiety, or any other issue which prevents them from meeting and connecting with someone in a healthy love relationship. Years have passed and they've become accustomed to being alone. Many of these people have physical needs since everyone was born with various ranges of sexual desire within them. This is also where pornography has been a positive. It helps that person use their imagination, or reach heights of sexual pleasure. They're not hurting anybody since they've been unable to connect with someone in any type of relationship.

A danger to abusing lust is you have a greater chance at attracting in and catching the variety array of STD's, or any other sexual related diseases that exist. The world witnessed this happen in massive numbers after the sexual revolution in the 1970's. Suddenly everyone was free, independent, and sleeping with endless partners, but then this insatiable uncontrollable lust caught up with them. Many started to witness their friends catching sexually transmitted diseases, or they saw them get their lives cut short due to other diseases such as the HIV virus. This is not the only way someone catches sexual related diseases. It is true that one can be promiscuous and yet they are severely disciplined in practicing safe sex precautions, while someone who is the opposite of that makes one slip and that slip is the time they caught something. However, the percentage of catching a disease is raised the more partners you engage with.

Where lust becomes a challenge with too much pornography is when someone would rather watch porn daily than connect with their lover. There are many couples who have a healthy sex life, and once in awhile the guy or girl watches porn. We don't want to stereotype that it's only men who watch porn, although traditionally men have been more known to watch or engage in porn than women as they tend to have a higher carnal sex drive. This is about the candidate who ignores their mate in order to lock their doors and watch porn alone day after day instead of connecting with a lover. Their mate has talked to them about connecting with them through affection, but it's repeatedly denied.

Sex and lust is everywhere you look now. Human life is bombarded by these images. Young people below the human legal age are also brought up in a world where this is in their face from an early age. This doesn't attribute to giving them a healthy view of sex when they grow older. It contributes to distorting their perception of human life while giving them low self esteem in the process. It also displays humankind has having no authentically deep connections around them. It's all about appearance, lust, and sex.

These picture perfect images of men and women looking flawlessly tight and packing it contributes to giving the masses low self-esteem when it comes to their looks. Endless studies have been conducted to show for example that men, as much as women, are dissatisfied with their appearance. These were cases where the candidates were asked about how they felt about muscle tone, weight issues, feeling judged by their looks, and pressured to look good. Nearly half the men surveyed admitted to being unhappy with their muscle tone, or they exercised solely to lose the extra pounds and not so much for health reasons. More than half of the men surveyed admitted to feeling judged by their looks or pressured to look like the hot model men do in magazines and online.

In these surveys, homosexual men scored slightly higher than heterosexual men in all categories. It is interesting to note the slight differences between heterosexual men and homosexual men and what propels them to feel more insecure about their looks and why. As past history and the media have indicated, women have always tended to feel insecure about their appearance. However, in more recent studies, it's showing that men equally feel this same insecurity as women. This is because the media and the Internet continue to bombard the masses with hot looking men and women in front of your eyes on a regular basis that it's no wonder everyone has become severely and inappropriately insecure about their appearance. The darkness of ego in the media promotes low self esteem to the world. This is not consciously, but when you have a raised consciousness, then you are aware of what you're contributing.

The one targeted area that men, both heterosexual and homosexual, have tried to cover up during sex is their stomach. This is not entirely surprising since they've been assaulted by an array of airbrushed images of other men having hard six pack abs in photos. Women and homosexual men lust after those abs, so this puts pressure on the guy to appear in a way that isn't realistic. They notice others constantly fawning and lusting over the hot sexy photos in the media that it gives them some measure of *body dysmorphic disorder*. This is where you find that you're constantly obsessing over some part of your appearance that you personally feel to be a major flaw.

More people are single than ever before in history, and there are a variety of factors why. One of them being that you are searching for that perfect flawless looking person that you will never obtain. It is impossible since no one is flawless. Even the good looking flawless ones are flawed. If they're not, their looks and appearance will still fade over time. This has made everyone have some measure of body dysmorphia. This isn't healthy on your self esteem or your life in general. You can see how the act of lust can blow up to the point where it infiltrates insecurities in the masses around the world desperately trying to look as good as possible to appear desirable to others.

You wake up and check your email and you are flooded by sexual images all over the Internet in front of you. You head on outside for a walk, and a hot guy or girl walks past you and smiles. You do a double take as you're physically attracted to them. Meanwhile, you're unaware this other person was thinking the same thing about you too. The lust quotient here begins to rise, since having an immediate physical attraction to someone is lust and not love. You are drawn to them physically and you feel that you need to have that person. Only after you've obtained that person in a long term relationship are you able to assess whether or not you have love for them. If after getting to know them, you feel nothing for this person months down the line, then this is a sign that you had a lust attraction for them, and were not in love with them.

Real honest love does not evaporate. Even if a couple separates or breaks up, they always have love for the other person even if it didn't work out in a relationship. If they have no love, then it's likely they never truly loved them, but were infatuated with them. This means it was a lust connection. The only reason one would lose complete love for someone they were involved with if it was real love, is if their ex-partner was abusive in any form or continuously hurt them. That will kick the love right out of you!

Some in a committed love relationship have announced that they're not turned on by anyone else other than their partner. While others may be loyal to their partner, but they check out other people on the street. They cannot help it because when someone sees beauty they want to stare at it. Looking is not cheating, although many partners will be bothered by it. You've seen this woven into endless movies where the one character is telling the other, "I saw you checking that person out! What was that about!?" It can be perceived as a threat or questionable, but not necessarily a cheat depending on who you talk to.

When men see someone attractive, it's like noticing a butterfly flitting past them, but then they're onto something else and no longer interested. They see someone who appears easy on the eyes to them and they do a double take. They cannot help it because the male perception is caught by beauty. It's harmless and nothing to be alarmed about. This is different than someone who takes it a step further beyond looking. They do whatever they can to capture that butterfly when they're supposed to be in a committed love relationship. This is when lust has taken over and now becomes a deadly sin challenge.

The most agreed upon infidelity crime committed is when someone kisses another person outside their relationship. With that said, you can understand that once someone takes it a step further and sleeps with another person outside the connection that the bond is now broken due to infidelity. Some see an emotional affair as cheating. This is where your partner grows exceedingly close to someone else emotionally. If they are someone who is heterosexual, then this person they're emotionally attracted to is of the opposite sex, and if they're homosexual, then it's the same sex. They may say the person is a friend and that is all it is, but there are cases where the intimacy starts out on an emotional level. Over time, it crosses the line into physical intimacy. Some find the emotional intimacy worse than the physical one. It is upsetting to discover their love partner has a deeper emotional connection with someone who is of a gender they are attracted to.

Psychologists have said that you can take anti-depressants to curb your sex addiction, but that's because anti-depressants diminish your sex drive. Those who need anti-depressants attempt to get off the medication due to the side effect that reduces ones sex drive. While someone who is a sex addict and wants to control it will get on anti-depressants to slow down their intense craving for all things connected to sex.

There are unreliable cases of what can lead to sex addiction since there isn't one way that the addiction comes about. Those who come from unloving homes tend to have a higher shot at becoming a sex addict. Neglect or sexual abuse at a young age can lead to sex addiction. There are the cases where someone becomes a sex addict because they have a higher sex drive than the average person. They channel it in a lust filled way. It's not something they can control or hold back necessarily.

There are also changeable levels of sex addiction. I've interviewed people who have explained they are always thinking sexual thoughts throughout each day. They are fantasizing up ways to climax. They typically crave a variety of partners to satisfy their desire for change and constant stimulation. Others will spend their days off surfing the internet for photos that are sexually related, which appeal to any personal fetish desires. They will watch pornographic videos and may even make their own amateur porn videos or performances for a web camera to onlookers. The rise of the internet and technology gave rise to everyone being stars in their own right. This includes being stars online through sex and pornography.

Technology is beneficial in that information travels faster. Two people can be on opposite sides of the world, and they are able to communicate as if they're neighbors living down the street from one another. It was intended to connect one another and assist in functioning more efficiently on the planet while here.

The electronic impulses in technological gadgets however can dim or cut off the communication line with Heaven. They are also used for narcissism and hate. This is seen through the "me-me-me" and "I-I-I" world. This is witnessed by the low vibration words posted in comments or social media on the web.

The darkness in one's ego takes these toys and becomes overly immersed in it by abusing it. It perpetuates lust through the media channels making humankind obsessed over someone's appearance. When someone dislikes someone or wants to find a way to attack, the not thought out way of attacking is by making a negative verbal remark on the person's appearance.

There are a couple of types of sex addiction. One of them is when you crave constant sex to feed a desperate desire for love. It is easier these days to find sex than it is to find love. You take what you can get. If love is not forthcoming, then you'll get it in any other way you can, even if the person you're sleeping with sees you as an object. You crave love and affection, and you've found another human being who will touch you so you go with it. Some of the cases I've received are where they are complaining that they are wrecked with lust filled desires. They will spend weeks sleeping with different partners and still feel lost. I've explained that they crave love and instead are hoping to find it through sex. Because a love relationship is not here, they have sex with those they do not care about instead. It temporarily fulfills them at that moment, but then the lust filled desire rises again the next day and they're out on the prowl for another conquest. They soon admit this to be true and open up about the love they crave that isn't present.

The other type of sex addiction is where you don't crave love at all, but you see other people as objects. If the object is beautiful, then you want to sleep with them, but you experience no emotional or even friendly attachment. When you're done having sex with them, then you leave and seek out another body to sleep with. When sex addiction moves beyond the craving, then it is an addiction to fulfill other hidden desires that have nothing to do with sex. This is the same way someone who has a food, drug, or alcohol addiction. It is to mask other feelings that need to be addressed and dealt with such as depression, stress, or anxiety. An addiction like any addiction happens in order to cover up or temporarily fulfill other emotional needs. An addiction is putting on a band aid to momentarily cover up a wound, but it doesn't heal the cut. It's a pain killer you continuously reach for in order to dull the pain.

Lust addiction can also be connected to love addiction where you always crave a love relationship. When you're finally in a relationship, you're looking for ways to get out of it, or you are secretly displeased with it. This is because it's not fulfilling your unrealistic views as to how a love relationship is supposed to be. You want it to be like it is in the movies. When it doesn't measure up, which most of the time it will not, then you want someone else instead. It's a cycle where your intimate connections with people are short lived.

The act of lust moves beyond love or sex addiction. Lust can be a super intense desire for someone who is completely wrong for you. They do not make you happy, and yet you hang onto them for dear life because you've developed passionate feelings for them. This other person you lust after has pulled away or is showing disinterest. This doesn't stop you from letting go of them. This is when the deadly sin of lust becomes a problem.

One reader named Denise reached out to me to explain how she met this guy named Steven who she was head over heels for. They spent six straight days together making love daily, but then they both had to go back to work. She was curious if this was the one.

I said, "Steven is not ready for a relationship. He's not looking for something serious right now. There is someone else with him too. Your connection with him won't last more than six months."

Denise said that Steven was a good looking bad boy body builder with tattoos. Denise had tattoos and was outgoing and considered the life of the party. When she confessed that she was in love with him after a month in I said, "You're not in love with him. You don't know him. You have lust for him because you think he's hot, but you don't know him well enough to be in love. Love is developed when you've known the person for at least a year. You've seen their flaws and challenges, and they've seen some of yours, and yet you both continue to care deeply for one another regardless."

Denise soon realized that Steven did not live in California. He lived in New York and would frequently visit California to do business and stay at Denise's place. She started to feel an imbalance in the connection. She later explained that she was the one buying the groceries, making their meals, driving him around while Steven rarely chipped in. The irony is that this was not a big enough red flag for her to dissolve the connection.

As the months progressed, she and Steven would fight and have endless hostile disagreements and arguments. He was insulting to her and would call her names. This is on top of the fact that he was using her to stay at her place while in town. He was saving a ton of money not having to stay at a hotel or rent a car, and she was feeding him so he had it made. She turned obsessive, co-dependent, and gushing whenever it came to him.

The notes I would receive from her were complaints about Steven. I said, "This doesn't sound like someone you love." She refused to let him go because she was lusting over him and his looks, but she didn't love him. How can you love someone who treats you horribly, uses you, and calls you names? By month six, the connection ended when she discovered he was indeed a player and had another woman around him.

In this scenario, Denise was governed by lust. You can see how that blinded the reality of the connection she was in. This is one way that lust can become a toxic challenge or sin. If you are immediately head over heels after meeting someone that is physically attractive to you, then you want to take caution that you do not become blindsided by who they truly are. Lustful eye candy can be deceitful to you if you're not careful in taking your time to get to know someone before you fall in too deeply. You're blinded by their beauty and the attention they're giving you by positively responding to your interest.

Sex is a major intoxication to masses of people around the world. In some countries, it is one end of the extreme where it's seen as forbidden and almost a crime. Whereas in other countries, it's the opposite extreme where it's become an obsession. The more skin you show, the more interest and popularity it garners. Everyone is ruled by sex to the point where it's an unhealthy blinding lust. It has become monotonous because there is no suspense, substance, or surprise.

When you see someone physically attractive or good looking, then you become all thumbs and dizzy losing your senses. I know, because I'm a love addict who sees and reacts to the beauty all around me. When super hot eye candy flits past you, then understand you're not the only one lustfully gazing upon this stunning creature. When you see someone who fits this description and you start talking, you either want to have sex with them or you want to date them and hope it'll lead to marriage. I've literally heard others say, "I want a hot husband/wife."

Where this becomes an issue is when you're blinded by their beauty and believe they are the one. Just because someone is good looking to you doesn't mean they would make a perfect lifelong mate. There are endless cases where two people couldn't be more incompatible, but one of them continues to push for it, because they're physically attracted to them. This is lust and not love, since love is developed over the course of time. In fact, in many of my studies and cases of couples who have gone the distance, they've admitted they were with someone who was not the type they were typically attracted to.

You want a healthy long term love relationship, but you're fixated on having that with someone you're overflowing with lust for. Physical attraction is an important aspect to consider in a love connection. The first thing you notice in a potential love partner is if you're physically attracted to them and vice versa. This physical attraction is lust. You sometimes start out with lust, but it is not something that guarantees a healthy long term love relationship. In fact, more times than not, those connections quickly dwindle away. There are other important traits that need to be factored in when it comes to a potential love relationship, such as similar interests, values, communication style, and needs.

Sometimes while deep in a love relationship, you realize your partner might have been heavily interested in the beginning, but gradually grew disinterested. Many are unable to continue past the newness of something or someone as time progresses. The odds are this person is like this with every relationship they're in.

I have a friend who is always hot and heavy immediately with someone new. He would quickly change his profile to *in a relationship*, within weeks of dating this new person. Within a month or two, his status would be changed back to *single*. There is a cycle going on in that scenario. He lusted after the new person, but as this person's flaws began to show, he grew bored with how this person looked. He never had true love for them to begin with since love lasts.

One of the big concerns others approach me about is love. Many frustrated people around the world wondering when it will happen for them. The upsurge of technology has played a part in crippling personal connections. Someone sends you a message on a phone app and they're sending that same message to a dozen others. Before apps and social media, when you met someone you treasured it. You took it seriously and built a strong lasting connection with them. Now you move on just as quickly as you start up.

Carnal pleasure is feeling a strong lust filled attraction to someone where you want to sleep with them, but there is no emotion or feeling involved. It's merely their physical appearance that appeals to you. It is possible to have both a lust filled and love connection with someone. This would be the best of both worlds for the romantic at heart. Many couples in long term love relationships have these strong passionate connections where it's both the lust and love intertwined.

In this sex driven world, it seems as if everyone is trying to climax. Countless people have been darting uncensored sexual words at one another. I've experienced this personally over the course of my life since I was a teenager. This especially took off with the rise of social media and phone apps.

My first book was lust filled and love related, yet I'm a much deeper soul than those coming onto me first realize. I'm not offended by the sexual words darted to me as if I'm an object. This is because nothing sex related offends me. Deep down it would bother me at times as it is not the way to get my attention let alone get me to climb into bed. Appeal to my mind, personality, and communication style. See me more than an object and have something to say other than sex. For many deep souls, this is what would make you turn your head and notice you. When you come at me by introducing yourself with obscene sexual words, then I'm bored and uninterested.

Sex became a big deal because it was seen by strong religious groups to be impure. God did not give you a sex drive in order to resist putting your hands down your pants. Loving yourself is self love and a way to release that pent up creative part of you. Indulging in physical pleasures becomes a problem when it consumes you and rules your life to the point where you have no honest soul connections with anybody.

The common theme with all of the deadly sins is similar to one another. It's basically excess and over indulgence in something, instead of moderation and self discipline. The obsession to crave something deeply consumes you and takes over your life to the point that you can no longer see straight. When you cannot see what's in front of you, then this carries over into other areas of your life. The adult sex world gives pleasure to those who are perpetually single and unable to connect with anyone whether it's a date or a romantic love relationship. When you fall too deep into the adult world where it's a daily obsession then it can block an incoming potential into your life. You forget how to communicate with others.

Healthy sex with the one you love is a luxury. Luxuries are a necessity to human life to keep from living in permanent stress or unhappiness. Partaking in fun activities that bring you joy are a great way to achieve this. This is the light side of lust because the act of luxury brings enjoyment, whereas lust is a heavy longing for something that brings on blindness. This blindness hides what one must see to keep from heading down paths that delay or corrupt the soul from achieving greatness.

Delight is another lighter form of lust because you are taking pleasure in pleasing someone else or yourself. It is done without effort or an uncontrollable craving. Delight is a high vibration feeling of joy and happiness, while a lust filled craving teeters on a lower vibration. You want what you cannot have or you're turning someone into an object rather than seeing the soul within them. Serial killers view others in this same manner as objects rather than a soul. Enjoyment is similar to the word *delight* where you get healthy pleasure from something. The lust action is that deep uncontrollable craving that borders on panic and anxiety that you need to have this or else.

Chapter Six

GLUTTONY

Gluttony is an excess of anything considered to be of waste. This includes overeating, addictions, and a strong appetite for clutter. You don't need seven cars if you're a millionaire or a disorderly home with junk piled sky high. When anything of material is hoarded, then this creates an imbalance in your life. Imbalance brings equal or greater disproportionate energy into your surroundings.

Some might hang onto their money out of fear. If you were someone who grew up poor, but then you grow older and become financially successful, then it's not uncommon to have the mentality engrained in your consciousness that you are poor. There is a dichotomy between the two extremes one might head down in this scenario. One is that you receive an increase in money gained, but you never touch it out of fear. The opposite extreme is spending it quickly and frivolously. Both excesses are connected to one living in a gluttonous way. It's the extremism or overindulgences that points to gluttony.

Actress, Angelina Jolie, has an estimated net worth of 140 million at this time. It has been said that she puts 1/3 of her money into savings, 1/3 towards charitable causes, and 1/3 towards living expenses. This is an example of one who balances out their income when it is excessively high. There are those who have a high amount of money who fearfully hang onto it as if they are broke. They might have millions of dollars in the bank, but their mindset is that of someone who is poor. All through their living days, they never part with it preventing a healthy flow of energy moving. One wealthy woman passed away and left her thirteen million dollars to her cat. This is another example of someone that lived a life of gluttony until she parted this world. A wise woman who has no one but her cat would ensure her money is disbursed equally through important humanitarian charities, those of low means, the poor, or anyone you're drawn to offer assistance to. Heaven looks to see if you have a giving nature in your heart. Those lacking in giving to others in some manner makes one gluttonous.

Celebrities get attacked by the public on a regular basis. The darkness of ego loves to negatively gossip about others, including those they don't personally know. When you dive into deeper research surrounding that celebrity, you discover the immense charitable causes they contribute large amounts of monetary assistance to. The one gossiping in a comment board about this person has contributed nothing positive to humanity in any way. They have committed the toxic sin of gluttony by gossiping in excess.

The traditional trait associated with gluttony is food. Food can become an addiction just like any other toxic vice. As a result it can make one become gluttonous. Overeating causes health issues that build up in your body over time. It blocks divine messages from seeping into your consciousness. It wears down your soul and makes you feel as if you're dragging along through each day even after eight hours of sleep. Overeating is especially dangerous when it comes to poor diets of foods that have zero nutritional value.

Gluttony became one of the deadly sins during a time when human souls were full of superstition. They equated gluttony to being a deadly sin and therefore against God's wishes. They claimed that the soul will be damned and punished when it crosses over. No one is going to be sent to Hell to burn for all eternity for sinning, but you are expected to learn from the mistakes you make in order for your soul's growth.

When you cross over, you move through a review process where the life you lived literally does flash before your eyes. You are shown every positive or negative choice you made in your life. It is revealed what you did to or for others. You are briefed on the accomplishments you made, and the ones that you agreed to make, but never did for various reasons. One of the reasons being that you denied the Heavenly guidance directing you repeatedly to do something. You ignored it or made excuses to avoid doing it, even though deep in your heart you felt a strong connection that it was something to pay attention to.

If you hurt someone, you experience this hurt yourself, as well as the pain the other person felt as a result. If you were someone who hurt dozens of people, then this is felt with all of them too. Imagine someone like Hilter and the life review he endured where he was moving through every single person he affected in a negative way. This is not just those that were killed, but that person's family and the survivors of that person as well.

The judgment coming upon you is the one that you place on yourself. You find that you are judging yourself for the ill will you caused on others. Your perception is broadened while back home in Heaven. You have a profound clarity that you wished you had while living an Earthly life. All souls have the capacity to have immense clarity while living an Earthly life. This is because you are born with this clear precision. When you raise your consciousness and take care of all parts of you, then this raises your vibration enabling you to be a crystal clear channel. You are aware and conscious of when you are stepping out of line with someone. You take necessary action steps to correct that immediately.

Heaven views the deadly sins as toxins that damage some part of yourself when used in abundance. During biblical days, it was said that eating sweets was a sin, because it leads to other sinful pleasures. It's not a sin, but over consumption of anything is toxic to your overall well-being.

Egotism is a dark form of Gluttony. This ties into self-importance, but when done in excess will turn others off. Appreciate all that you are, shout it from the rooftops, and all over your social media page, but it will turn into overkill when it's done in excess. While some of us love to gloat about ourselves every chance we get, sometimes it's best to shake that up a little by turning the spotlight onto something or someone else in an encouraging way. You can do that by boasting on about it in a positive way. Post meaningful words that can inspire or help others once in awhile. Mix that with the self-important, "Look how great I am", stuff. This is all about maintaining balance in your life.

While gloating on about oneself every waking minute is not exactly harmful, it can bore and turn others off. Narcissism was a word created to be used as a semi-insult against someone who cares about themselves way too much. We say 'semi' because the narcissus typically doesn't care if you think that's what they are or not.

I've learned from my own Spirit team that there is nothing immoral with stroking your own ego....to a degree. One should take heed when it feels as if it's become overload or gluttonous. Like all of the deadly sins, this becomes a problem when it's in excess. If one is conceited, then this adds those blinders, which prevent you from seeing your life path more clearly .

Materialism is aligned with gluttony and egotism.

It's one of the most dominate traits that exist in humankind today. This is a world that has taught others to crave, desire, and long for material based items. You need to have that new phone or new computer release before anyone else has it. You have to wear the best designer clothes on your back, drive the best car, and live in the most magnificent house. Materialism is a force that blocks out heavenly guidance. It allows little to no room for light to enter in. Materialism is the opposite of the higher self's goal and interest. It's not aligned with a raised consciousness of your spirit. Those wading in an area of non-belief of anything outside of themselves are more than likely attracted to materialism. When you're heavily caught up in the tornado of materialism, then you're vastly unaware that you are.

Materialism is like wearing a gigantic blindfold over your eyes. These are the ones who regularly obsess about their job, money, home, car, physical looks, etc. Security is a desire that most everyone wants, but it's asked that you keep that contained. Avoid allowing it to consume who you are. It consumes you when it's all you think about. This thinking about it has a fear energy attached to it. The longing desire for security creates a block as mentioned in the lust chapter. It's the longing feeling that is a low vibration causing that which you do not want to come into your life. You're saying, "Please bring me this thing, which I do not want." The obsession over material items directs heavy focus on a physical possession, which carries no positive energy.

Consumption of anything in grand quantities is what brings on blocks from the Divine. Excess leads to health issues and life complications. Gluttony is when you periodically consume high amounts of food when there are starving people in the world that could use assistance.

Glutton is not a word used in the modern day world, but it was an archaic word used regularly during biblical days to describe an excess of food consumption. The meaning is still alive and well today even if the materialistic world is unable to see it. They are too close to the epicenter of materialism to have an understanding of the detriment it causes on your consciousness.

Over consuming anything can be connected to emotional issues. Toxic foods desired are cutely called, "*Comfort Foods*", because it gives the person emotional comfort through food. You desire comfort foods to offer a cushion or numb the emotions you're feeling. This is the same way one reaches out for alcohol, drugs, or any other toxic vice to numb emotional pain. There has been a long running epidemic of people abusing toxins so severely. Most of it is because they can't take it anymore. They can't take Earthly life and the people in it. They are so sensitive and in tune with Heaven more than they realize, but will dull it through pills or any other vice.

Many parts of the world have a higher obesity rate than others. Some of that is due to thyroid issues or metabolism speed. Another reason is due to the over consumption of food high in calories and saturated fat. This is accompanied with little to

no regular physical movement or exercise.
Exercise is not high on the lists of some due to laziness. The other reason it's avoided is you're overworked with no time. This is thanks to the break your back until you die mentality that the work force has hammered into the psyche of so many souls. They're too exhausted to go for a jog or head to the gym after another ten to twelve hour day that includes getting ready for work, sitting in traffic, sitting at work all day, then getting back into your car in traffic, and heading home to make dinner. Boom the day is gone. You head to bed and repeat. There is little to no personal or exercise time. Exercise is one of the top instructions Heaven has given me since I was a teenager. They want you take care of the vessel you are renting for a limited time while here. When you take care of yourself inside and out, then you have more time and energy to connect with loved ones and to put towards your life purpose. You are also a clearer psychic vessel able to pick up on the Heavenly messages and guidance coming in.

Gluttony can also be an excess of work. As mentioned, many in the world have this break your back mentality in their work life. This excess has killed their life force. It's noticed when you cross paths with them. Their aura is surrounded by a dark, sad, heavy, tiredness. Some are predominately stressed, dejected, miserable, and angry. They drive and back forth to work every morning and night as if their life depended on it. Heaven is a strong proponent of hard work, but working five to seven days a week, ten to twelve hours a day is not working hard. It's called *poor time management.*

You may think you're working an eight hour day, but you're not when you factor in the time you wake up to get ready, sit in traffic to and from work, and then your lunch hour. It's anywhere between nine to twelve hours each day by the time you add it all up. This leaves little to no room for taking care of yourself and those around you. Multiply that by day, week, month and year. It's no wonder human souls age at an accelerated rate mixed in with an underlying bitterness. This has become a major issue in the modern day world, which is why this is something my Spirit team has been talking to me about more than ever before now.

My Spirit team had me discuss the implementation of a *Four Day Work Week* in my book, *Darkness of Ego.* Many European countries have made note that the current work life schedule is not practical or healthy on ones well being. These are countries such as the Netherlands, Ireland, Denmark, Belgium, Norway, Italy, Switzerland, Germany, Sweden, and add Australia to the list. Switzerland in general has been known to have some of the happiest people around. They make the same amount per year as the average American, but they work less hours than them.

These countries listed for the most part implemented shorter work day schedules that increase productivity and give employees more personal time to take care of themselves and connect with family, friends, and loved ones. This helps to boost morale and make people happier.

When people are happier, they work harder and get the same amount of work done in a shorter amount of time. A work-a-holic would scoff at this, but check to see how they're doing health wise. Besides, I've always been a bit of a work-a-holic myself, but this is because I don't do well with idle time. If there is time to spare, I find ways to fill it with something. But these are things I do for myself to continue to improve me. When you work smart, then you have more energy and optimism to accomplish other things.

Having great time management skills means organizing the choices you make on any given day to ensure you're able to sufficiently include important tasks. You have an important deadline for a project that needs to get done. Do you have time to squeeze in a fifteen minute bike ride, a brisk walk, or a jog? Efficient time management enables you to break up your tasks into smaller pieces so that everything gets done in the same day. This can be from a little bit of exercise, attention to the project at hand, as well as make dinner, and connect with family, loved ones, and friends.

Sometimes too much time is spent on one particular task or duty. It not only dulls the quality of the project you're focused on, but there is no time to squeeze anything else in such as rest and relaxation activities. Other ineffective ways that crush time management is falling into the habit of time wasters, such as internet surfing for no reason, gossip, taking long personal lunch breaks that last for hours.

I met an Indian woman who worked her entire

life in an accounting department. When I met her she was at the end of her rope in her seventies. She was haggard, moody, stressed, and depressed. She was let go from her position, but she told me she saw it as a blessing in disguise. We would communicate here and there over the course of a year after that. When I saw her in person after a year I noticed this enormous glowing uplifting energy around her.

I mentioned that to her and she smiled excitedly, *"I am so happy. I've had more time for rest and exercise. I exercise every single day now because I have more energy. My husband has cut down on his drinking. Before when I was working all day, I'd come home stressed and tired and just want to go to bed. Now that I'm around, he's happier and uninterested in heavy drinking. He's said he doesn't feel driven to drink as much anymore."*

This isn't saying, "Everyone quit your job!" This woman had worked her entire adult life and was ready for retirement. This is about not working in excess. No one should be working five days a week, ten hours a day. That exhaustive run down kind of work is no longer necessary. There are some exceptions such as in the film industry. When you're filming a movie for a studio you are working in excess of twelve hours a day. This is because there are millions of dollars at stake in the movie business. However, when the movie is over, then the employment is over. You can choose to take two months off if you want after that before accepting another film production gig.

It is one thing to find meaningful work you're passionate about where it doesn't feel like a job to you. But most people work for the man as they say, or the corporate world, and no one is happy. I've worked in the job force for over two decades and had rarely come across a happy person. Even if the person is happy, they still appear worn out and unhappy underneath. You pick up on that permanent exhausted energy in their aura.

The light side of Gluttony is temperance. This is partaking in things in moderation and showing self-restraint. This is bringing balance into all areas of your life. It's okay to have a piece of that chocolate cake once in a blue moon, but not every night. It is okay to want the hottest computer or that great new phone, but it's not what governs you. You're not in a desperate feeling state where you're willing to stand in a six hour line to get it. That same phone will still be there and available a week later. It doesn't need to be a life or death longing.

When you find you've fallen down the path of gluttony, then shake it up by displaying selfless compassion to others. When you find passion in putting in work to assist humanity in positive ways, then that reduces your need to consume toxins in excess.

Chapter Seven

WRATH

The act of wrath is connected to an expression of venomous anger that causes you to lash out aggressively against someone. There are different levels of this anger as there are with all of the toxic challenges. It's a natural reactive emotion to rise to anger when someone is abusing the planet, children, animals, or any part of humanity in any form. The wrathful anger with the deadly sins is someone who is abusive towards others. It's especially vengeful when it's done to someone who caused no one harm, rather than you enacting wrath out of self defense. Wrath is taking the hate to the next level in a revenge scenario.

It is called a crime of passion when a woman tries to run over her husband with a car because he cheated on her, or a man murders his wife for committing infidelity. The crime of passion phrase is disguising the fact that one reacted to something they discovered with wrath like anger.

Day to day life can bring out wrathful anger in the most innocent person who is typically a peaceful being, but pushed beyond their limit. Wrath can be someone who is horn happy in their car because their ego is bruised over someone cutting them off in traffic. One of the worst forms of wrath is a terrorist murdering people. The terrorist does not believe in the personal values that the victim holds. This goes against God and all in Heaven making wrath one of the greatest and dangerous sins of all. It results in taking someone else's life, which is against God's law.

Friday, December 13, 2015, the world was shaken up when a band of terrorists committed violent crimes killing and injuring hundreds of innocent people in Paris, France. This is an example of the darkness of ego in top form. Unfortunately, that was only the beginning and these terrorist groups will continue to grow and expand. The world has always been at war over the centuries of evolution. The planet has never been balanced thanks to those filled up with wrathful darkness in their souls. The hostility of the planet appears to be particularly keen because of the rapid way that information travels through the universe online. It is no worse today than it was during biblical times. The difference is that the public never heard about it pre-media days. There weren't as many people on the globe then as there are at this time. The wrathful violence has multiplied to some degree because there are more people on the planet. With more people, comes more vengeance. This is also why there are a great deal of souls choosing to incarnate into an Earthly life from their realm home in Heaven. They are here for specific purposes that contribute to bringing light to this hostile planet. Peace is desired deep down in the heart of one's true soul, but it is a struggle for many to obtain with all of the tampering physical influences knocking you off balance.

Those who have incarnated from a realm have a big job going to battle with those who operate primarily from the darkness of their ego. Some of the top beasts that contribute to the darkness are those who post negative comments or reviews online. The other offenders are the media, specifically gossip media. Neither should be allowed to have access to a computer to spread venom. They're not old enough for that kind of responsibility.

It is true that the masses amount of dark ego energy being emitted into the air contribute a great deal to the Earth's density, but they are not the sole contributor. The Earth's atmosphere is already dense to begin with. It would be less dense without the darkness of human ego on the planet.

This particular terrorist attack in Paris France, along with most terrorist attacks, was religious driven by misguided dark souls. Misguided because they are convinced their personal prophet or God is instructing them to enact this violence. The information they are hearing come from the dark ego in man, and not God, since God only communicates in love and would never tell someone to kill another. The voices that instruct you to hate or kill another come from your ego. No hatred of any kind exists with God.

There will be more carefully arranged orchestrated attacks by terrorist groups. Terrorists are ecstatic over how successful their killings are. They love that the world gets upset and bothered by it. They don't operate the way everyone else does. Their consciousness is terribly low that it resides in a state of delusion. It is one that views human life as disposable.

Many lose faith when they witness others behaving badly. They understandably have questions about human existence and God. The Paris attacks are nothing compared to the other atrocities that will be coming. God is not allowing circumstances like this to happen, and it's not for His entertainment. Neither He nor any other spirit being can stop people from committing heinous acts. They can warn human souls or guide them away from committing these acts, but if one is not paying attention to God and their Guides and Angels, then there is only so much they can do. Those on the other side do their best to stop someone from desiring to inflict harm on themselves or others before ones time. The darkness in that soul is so far gone and blocked that the individual has no crystal clear connection with God at all. Those souls are not in tune to something greater than them. They are not paying attention to Heavenly guidance. The dangerous delusion is that they believe they are.

Heaven can protect those who communicate

with them and request their help, but no one did in this unfortunate Paris attack. The attacks also took place in an area that is packed with people. When you're absorbing others tampering energies, then this can dim the communication line with God. This is unavoidable since you cannot live in fear. It is a luxury to go out and have a good time pending that it's not hurting anyone. This is explained to illustrate some of the circumstances that caused these blocks within the human soul preventing them from picking up on Divine communication.

There was alcohol being consumed, and alcohol in high quantities blocks the communication line with Heaven. You've got tons of people's energies in one space, and alcohol prevented all of those people from picking up on that something wasn't right. This doesn't make it okay, but warnings were implemented into their consciousness. This is why its insisted that people be as clear-minded as possible.

This is never in judgment, because I love a good concert, glass of wine, or cold beer, but I do know when I'm in those situations, the communication line is dimmer than usual. I shield myself in protection on a daily basis and I also pray daily. This is not a standard practice by most in today's world, and in fact a non-believer would likely roll their eyes at all of this, let alone pick up a book like this to begin with.

All spirit souls have an ego except for the Angels and Archangels. The ego is expanded while in a human body and in the Earth plane. Terrorists are baby souls, meaning they have never had a human life before. They were spawned out of the light and immediately were born into a human physical body for their first life run. It's expected they would learn to expand their consciousness while here, but instead chose to follow the path of their dark ego.

The media is typically all over the place so you cannot rely on them to give accurate information. It is also mostly not objective, but has hints of where the journalist stands personally. Terrorists spend every waking moment planning, plotting, and acting. They're not going to stop as long as members exist. They know the weaknesses of humankind and will strike in places that no one expects them to. Malls and shopping centers are an easy target. Security is relaxed if even existent in those areas. There are more people congregated in malls, promenades, and shopping centers who are not expecting an attack. They go about their business shopping since the odds of anything happening are indeed slim. Terrorists do not have a consciousness and are not fearful of anything. They have cocky arrogance and witness situations such as what happened in Paris as a success. They couldn't wait to take credit for it. The light must face this darkness head on and wipe out all traces of evil.

Heaven says that Earth is a school and a place of learning for the soul. The ego expands as easily as the soul's light does while living an Earthly life.

Souls agree to an Earthly life to endure positive and challenging experiences. These experiences contribute to expanding, growing, and evolving the soul. The ego tests you in order to help you become accustomed to controlling it by smartening up. You do this by learning to pay attention to all that is around you. Learn to treat others with respect and love, pending they are respecting you. When you are disrespected, then you train the soul the meaning of the words love and respect. School yourself in understanding that you are a soul in a human body and that all of these physical distractions around you are just noise. The world has witnessed spiritual gurus or Buddhists put themselves through rigorous metaphysical training to become detached to the drama and unnecessary triviality around them, then the soul can move to higher dimensions and destinies.

The view from Heaven is there is no death the way some on Earth believe death to be. Heaven is saddened to see dark souls behave the way they do. To view a soul that grew out of touch with its reality is a depressing sight. Many souls are out of touch and not connected as it is. They're obsessed with what's going on in the physical world and with each other. Many have no faith in anything beyond this world. They are interested in naively taking the deadliest sins to the extreme through greed, envy, lust, sloth, gluttony, pride, or wrath. All of these are blocks from becoming a stronger and more powerful soul.

Wielding a knife or a gun at someone else doesn't make you powerful. It makes you weak hiding behind something that you feel will make you powerful and in control. People do this when they join cults, gangs, or even religious institutions. It's to feel as if they have some purpose by being backed and supported by their peers. It's a shield to hide behind to give one the illusion of power, when in fact it is the opposite. You rely on groups and your peers to boast you up instead of working on soul enhancing exercises to stand strong on your own by displaying love, assertiveness, and compassion. Stand in your own individual power even if others disagree.

Some want to remove blocks to be more psychic and be able to tell the future, but that's not the main reason anyone should desire to remove blocks. Fortune telling has a probable percentage of coming true since most human souls act out on free will. This shifts the probable outcome when one gets a clairvoyant vision of the future. Removing blocks opens up these communication lines with the individual soul's team, so when a warning of danger is dropped into their consciousness, then they can extricate themselves out of there. If they are a murdering terrorist with some kind of vengeful wrath and vendetta, then they will pick up on that guidance to stop and turn their life around in a positive way.

Terrorists have wrathful vengeance in their soul. Wrath, like all of the deadly sins, blocks the communication to line to God. So in essence, terrorists are not acting out God's plan, but their own darkness of ego plan. They are too blocked to see clearly and refuse to expand their consciousness and do the work of becoming a stronger soul. Had spiritual soul enhancing exercises been taught to them while in grade school or at home, then they would've gone down a much richer and loving path than the vile one they're currently stuck in. Many dark souls that remain stuck in this life are stuck in the transition portal into the next life when they pass on. It's one dark black hole where the light is avoided and not reached. It's not uncommon for the dark soul to go through a boomerang effect where they travel through darkness not reaching the light, and instead darted back around and into another human birth in hopes the soul will get it right. The life circumstance they're born into is worse than the one they just completed. This is for soul enhancing reasons.

The world witnesses human souls behaving badly and it's God who is blamed, but the only ones wreaking havoc are the human souls themselves. It's not His fault since He is not the one doing these things. Man is. God may have created the planet and the universe, but he didn't invent beer, guns, buildings, cars, computers, phones and other distractions that have cut off the God supply and the communication line to Heaven. These are all human made luxuries and in some circumstances a necessity. Taking these things to the extreme or abusing it will put up a barrier between you and God.

Tragedies should serve as a reminder of how desperately peace on Earth is needed. Many in the world are sick of it and want it to stop. A catastrophe happens on the planet and acts as a wake up call, then everyone joins together in solidarity. It becomes a hot trending topic online, but then days or even weeks of it being the biggest news story, the world gets back to their lives and forgets all about it until the next big catastrophe is brought to light to talk about. The world cares for a minute and then moves on to another hot story.

There are super dark souls threaded among humankind causing tons of problems on fellow human beings. Some of them are these murdering terrorists, but this darkness is also threaded among innocent souls as well through bullying and antagonizing those around them. Bullying and antagonizing fall into the Wrath category. They have internal anger to harass or harm someone else for no conscious reason. This is present all over the media, social media, and wherever comment forum boards exist.

Faith declines when you witness violence and hate happening around you. You question God and this Earthly existence. Avoid allowing your faith to waver, and know that blessings are bestowed following a tragedy. Don't let setbacks and violence knock down your faith. Let it make you stronger. You've got to stand strong in the face of adversity. You cannot allow it to crumble you. Those filled with hate cannot conquer you or the world. They may create a mess, but they will never win.

After the Paris attacks, a French artist, made a statement through an art drawing that more or less thanked people around the world that prayed for Paris, but he made a point to add that the country does not need more religion.

This is an example of when the ego has been consumed and influenced by human physical life fads, trends, and the media. Prayers are positive thoughts and not resorted to those who are religious. Atheists and non-believers are praying without realizing it. When you sit quietly with your thoughts and adjust them to something positive, then you are praying. Praying is more than kneeling down in a Church with your hands clasped together. This example and statement is intended to debunk the naïve myth that praying is only resorted to the religious. Statistically its appeared that the majority of the terrorists that chose to take another human life did so as a result of their religion. This gives religion a bad name by influencing others to view all religion as bad. There are good and bad people in every group, including the religious and the non-believers.

Serial killers dominated Earth's history mostly in the United States before technology. They were meticulous in their killings and tended to be Caucasian mid-to-late 30's and beyond. This changed post technology when they were no longer called serial killers, but deranged young men with psychological problems. The killings that would take place would be young men in their twenties going on a shooting spree. It's almost as if the culture was breeding these murdering trends. If these guys had the proper attention from others they probably wouldn't have fallen off the deep end. There are female serial killers, but it is typically male. Men are taught to repress emotion, which is not natural. It's not aligned with the soul's capabilities, and therefore the emotion and ways they're trained to behave builds until it erupts. Now serial killers are called the more glamorous title of "Terrorist".

Gossip is not listed as one of the seven deadly sins, but it does fall into having no self control, which is connected to the sin of greed. It is also connected to the sin of wrath, since the energy of gossip has the goal of attacking and antagonizing others even if it's in a passive aggressive manner. Some are unaware they've fallen into gossip, because gossip feels like a drug rush high to the ego. This creates blinders over the higher self suddenly ignorant to the real truth. Gossip is bullying and making accusations about someone you know nothing about. It is equal to physical violence, except this time the violence is with words. When it's provoking enough it will push the ego to act out in wrathful physical violence. This has been seen with violent protestors and the lynch mob of the world. They disagree with someone or something, then they want to do anything they can to see that person get killed. The hatred they have in their hearts is equal to the sin of wrath and causes them to gossip.

Entertainer Michael Jackson was accused for the crime of sexual molestation in the early 1990's and again in the early 2000's. The media and the dark side of human ego gossiped about it for years and some indefinitely throughout their lives. What the media and the public failed to mention was that Michael Jackson was never proven guilty. It turned out that in reality he was taken advantage of by a couple of families that he had graciously allowed into his home. These families were only interested in gaining some of Jackson's fortune. Through the sin of greed they were going to do everything in their power to obtain this money including through slander. People will do whatever they can to obtain something as mentioned in the greed chapter.

The media never reported on Michael's innocence or about how the case files were laid out and concluded. The media and public only focused on the dirty slanderous gossip made about Michael Jackson. Once again the darkness of ego proved that it's easily led like cattle. One person says something erroneously untrue about someone and another around them picks it up and goes along with it and so forth.

One of the reasons the media doesn't report on how a case like this ends is because it's not titillating or exciting. "Awe, we're sorry, we were wrong. It turns out he was innocent."

If a case ends positively in favor of the one they made a victim out of, then the media is hush about it. It's not exciting enough to the ego who prefers sensationalized drama to incite lynch mob violence.

It's easier to gossip about something you know nothing about rather than pouring through endless research on case files to come to the truth. The tragedy is not only the lives it's harmed in the process, but that this dark behavior has been going on for centuries. How about the Salem Witch Trials in the late 1600's? People were being accused of witchcraft by gossips. As a result, those accused were put to death in various ways. It later turns out they were wrongfully accused and executed. Years droned on as the human souls of the Light tirelessly worked to make things right for the victims wrongfully murdered as well as their families. This same behavior by the gossips who made these accusations is still going on centuries later. As Saint Nathaniel has told me in past connections, humankind is super slow to evolve.

Officer Darren Wilson was accused of murdering Michael Brown in 2014 in Ferguson, Missouri. Wilson said it was self defense, but witnesses said that Michael Brown asked him not to shoot him. This set out a public lynching against Darren Wilson and caused the Ferguson Riots. Years later and after much investigation by authorities and the courts, it turns out the witnesses lied under oath and everything that those rooting for Michael Brown said turned out to be false. Yet, as per usual, the media did not ensure that the public knew this truth. This case caused unnecessary riots created out of the tantrum of the dark ego in humankind.

These are all examples of wrathful gossip by the darkness of ego. Steer clear of gossip and avoid blindly following the herds of those who do not know much. If masses of hysteria and sensationalism are riding sky high, then this is clue to detach from that energy and stay away from it. Tune in to your higher self, God, and your Spirit team in order to come to the highest truth without judgment.

Sensitive and in tune human souls cannot witness horrible attacks on others. If this is you, then you are highly connected to the other side. And with that comes absorbing both the light and the darkness around you. Catastrophes and the violence showcased in the media daily can wear your system out. Detach and remove yourself from any areas around you that will perpetuate this drama. This includes friendships that are full of gossip. Avoid reading sensationalized news pieces. Be able to tell the difference if a piece is objective or prone to gossip.

The world needs to unite as one. These continuing violent incidents human kind incites are no accident. It is time for the world to wake up and band together and support and love one another. The endless fighting has been going on for centuries getting everyone nowhere. Throughout history all of the power struggles, bloodshed, the murders, and the fighting has never brought anyone peace. When you have wrath in your heart, then you are blocked from the Divine. Work on centering yourself in peace and patience, instead of lashing out in an attack.

Chapter Eight

SLOTH

$\mathcal{A}$ sloth is a lazy person who refuses to put in an effort and get to work on anything. It can be someone who is a slacker, emotionally dead, or apathetic. When you're emotionally disconnected, then this can hurt elements of your existence. Relationships suffer greatly with the sloth as the sloth tends to be disconnected from their partner. This puts strain on the connection by building a wall between them until the two separate and break apart. The sloth lacks in passion in many areas of their life. This is different than practicing emotional detachment. Emotional detachment is when you have a vast reservoir of feeling, but you have an indifferent aloofness to other people's drama. Emotional detachment is a smart protection device in order to avoid absorbing the toxic emotions of others into your aura. When someone acts out of selfish desires to fulfill personal needs, then it affects loved ones and eventually backfires.

When you experience permanent laziness, an inability to work, improve yourself and this world in some manner, then this opens the door to toxic addictions. You are apt to getting into trouble, or consuming high amounts of toxins due to boredom and idleness. Over the years, I've witnessed hardworking people at their job, but when they have a day off they wake up and begin the process of consuming one alcoholic drink after another. This continues until it's finally time to go back to work. This is a result of being unhappy or overworked. When one is happy and not permanently exhausted, then they are less likely to drink alcohol all day whenever they have a day off.

I was one of those people during the first half of my twenties while working in the film business. During the film production tenure of my entertainment industry life, I would be working 12 hours plus a day, five days a week, for months. Incredibly hardworking, on the mark, highly demanded, and sought after by Hollywood talent. Yet, when Friday night would roll around, I would become the opposite of that. I'd hang out with my friends holding a bottle of wine in my hand drinking late into the night until I passed out or blacked out. You spend the next day hung over and the only way to get rid of that was have another drink.

With the assistance of Heaven and my Spirit team, I gradually reduced or dissolved the various addictions I was consuming in toxically high quantities, including alcohol. I remember some would later ask, "Why did you stop drinking like that?" I half joked, "I got tired of losing a day."

I only had a limited time off on the weekends and I was growing tired of wasting it in a haze. I wanted to be clear minded and present in order to enjoy the days off. I also have a huge industrious creative gene that screams for productivity every second.

Drinking in excess is rejected by the body as a toxin. Having a drink or two a day is not going to kill you. It may even have an added benefit as some health reports have indicated, but this is about those who continue drinking throughout the day until they're slurring their words. Some gain a sharp tongue while on many drinks. Loved ones in the line of that fire listen to the heavy drinker rambling on about nothing that makes any sense. Or they are verbally attacked by the heavy drinker. This causes them to lose an attraction to the person. The drinker wakes up the next day and has no idea why their loved one is suddenly distant. Or they get into trouble by falling down a path of lust filled addictions. They begin chatting on sex apps, meeting people, going to the bar to hang in all night. Not only does this taint your character, but it pushes away loved ones around you, and blocks divine communication. When you're in that mind space, you have no compassion for who you're doing that to. You don't care, which makes you a sloth.

The next day after a night of drinking, I'd call a

friend up, "Did I say anything bad last night?"

They'd say, "No you were fine, but then again, I was out of it too, so I'd be the last person to ask."

I worried about what I was saying to people rather than what I did. As my past history has shown, those around me confirmed I was a fun drunk. Or they'd say with a huge smile insinuating something, "You certainly had fun last night!"

I'd shake my head brushing it off, "No, this isn't good. I can't keep doing this."

Luckily, with the assistance of my Spirit team, I was able to reduce my alcohol intake. I say reduce instead of eliminate, because I still have a drink or two from time to time, but it's not something I crave. I can go for months without one. Whereas in my twenties, it was let me drink one after the other until I can no longer stand up. I did a turnaround one month and a half before my twenty-seventh birthday. This was when being clear minded, active, and productive shot to the top of my list and permanently stayed there. I've lived in the trenches of addiction and understand what it's like first hand. I know what it's like to battle an addiction and struggle to get out of it and achieve it. Unhappiness on any level in your life drives you to a toxic addiction. This isn't suggesting that there is something wrong with you if you enjoy your glass of wine every night. What I was doing in my early twenties was ten times more excessive than the occasional drink a night.

The lazy person is vilified by all around them from friends, family, lovers, and employers. The sloth is someone who takes advantage of others, humanity, the system, and the government. They are capable of putting in an effort and being productive, but instead will look for ways to abuse that by relying on money from any source beyond putting in the work. This money ultimately comes from those who are hardworking and putting in an effort. Hard workers might unknowingly be aware that they are supporting the sloth. This is not about someone with a disability that prevents them from being able to work. This is about the person who is perfectly capable of putting in the work, but doesn't feel like it.

The sloth can also be someone who is gifted, but does nothing with those talents. This is like the character from the movie, *Good Will Hunting*. Will Hunting is a tough young man in Boston who grew up in an abusive household. He aggressively confronts anyone in his path that he feels is a threat, but he is also a genius able to solve difficult mathematical problems. What makes him a sloth is that he chooses to work as a laborer instead of doing something with his gifts and talents. Everyone around him notices this genius quality about him and they watch him in awe.

At one point his best friend, Chuckie, confronts Will. Chuckie explains to Will that every morning he picks him up so they can carpool to work together. Chuckie confesses that he secretly wishes that one day he would go to pick Will up, but Will is nowhere to be found. He has moved away in order to do something grand with his life. Chuckie admits that he'll personally be a laborer the rest of his life, but Will is gifted and if he doesn't do anything with that, then it would be a great disappointment to him. In this scenario, Chuckie acts as soul mate to Will since soul mates are put in your path to push your buttons and help you improve. They challenge you and hold up a spotlight on stuff you do not want to face. This is for your own good.

In the end, Will evolves out of sloth mode and follows his best friend's advice. Chuckie goes to Will's front door one morning to pick him up for work, but discovers for the first time that there is no answer. He smiles to himself knowing that his best friend is going to do something great with his life.

When one develops their gifts and talents or puts it to positive use, then the sloth part of them dissolves away.

One of my lifelong best friends had commented after seeing *Good Will Hunting* that Will had reminded him of me. This was back when I was twenty-six and drinking myself into a stupor. My friend said something to me that forever embedded itself into my consciousness.

"Will Hunting reminds me of you. You're extremely tough and don't take anything from anyone. You grew up in an abusive household like Will. And yet you're incredibly gifted more than you realize. Like Will's friend, I've sometimes thought to myself that one day you don't pop by my place. And this is because you've taken off to do something great with your talents."

He later witnessed that take place with me over the years and performing that turnaround and into an advocate and spokesperson for improving oneself on all levels.

Sloth like behavior is when you move through a long period of inactivity. Most everyone has experienced this at some point in their life. There can be factors that propel this to happen such as depression or stress. The sloth can be the human soul that lacks any kind of motivation or is against work of any kind. Heaven loves those who work hard. This is not to be confused with the work-a-holic or the soul who is driven by work for the sole purpose of money.

Heaven praises the hard working soul, but they also insist that you balance that with relaxation and personal time. The sloth is someone who is indefinitely lazy. They are always lounging around, watching television, or surfing the internet aimlessly every day. They are also the ones sitting behind their computer posting toxic negative comments into the universe. The sloth's work history is minimal if at all, because they're not productive. They are not the ones going out there to try and find work, or helping others in a positive way. The sloth might also be the person who has a job, but they do the bare minimum if anything at all.

Heaven sees the sloth person as the one more

likely to get into trouble for having too much time on their hands. When Heaven says they love hard working souls, this doesn't mean run out and get a corporate 9-6 job. They are talking about the souls who are also doing something positive to contribute towards humanity. If they are out of work, they're still getting out there, getting exercise, finding positive activities to partake in. The sloth is the one who might never leave their house out of sheer laziness, and not because they have social phobias. The sloth is a lazy person who is indefinitely unmotivated to challenge themselves.

It's natural to feel sluggish from on occasion. Even the most energetic enterprising human soul is going to hit a wall now and then. This feeling is your body telling you to take a break. The sloth takes a permanent break that lasts for years.

The *Little Red Hen* is a fairy tale story designed to engrain proper ethics to Children. It tells the fable of a little red hen who told the other farm animals that she was going to bake some bread. She asked who would help her throughout the process. All of the animals would say, "Not I."

When the bread was finally completed, she asked who would help her eat it. Naturally all of the animals said, "I will!"

She informed them that they would not help her eat it. She was going to eat it herself since no one bothered to lift a finger and help her during the productive stages of making the bread. The other animals in this scenario are an example of a sloth.

It is typical human behavior by many to not be interested in putting in the work, but still be handed gifts. The sloth is never rewarded. If that appears to not be the case, then those gifts will eventually be taken away at some point. This is due to the law of Karma that the energy you put out there is darted back to you eventually.

The sloth is also someone who becomes apathetic or indifferent to basic spiritual values. They are disconnected from their own soul and anything that is outside of the physical world. It is someone whose life force has diminished.

This was the seed that prompted me to write the book, *Ignite Your Inner Life Force*. I spent the previous year watching my life force weaken due to the crumbling of a love relationship I was in. The after effects included no longer caring about anything. I became indifferent, disconnected, and numb to everything around me. I knew that state would not last forever, and that I would need to get back to business. I had regular talks with my team that we would need to work on re-igniting my life force and bring me back. Living in sloth mode is a terribly depressing state to be in. The book became the beginning of the next chapter of my life. This is an example of moving yourself out of sloth mode and back into passionate productivity.

We've looked at some of the ways the sin of the sloth plays a role in the lives of so many people. This includes the obvious, which is extreme perpetual laziness and lethargy.

One girl in her twenties was collecting unemployment checks. She told her friends, "Why should I look for a job when they're only going to pay me the same amount that I make on unemployment?"

This is an example of someone who has fallen into sloth mode. They take advantage of the system and prefer to have blessings handed to them without putting in the work.

From another perspective, one can look at it from her point of view. Why should she work a job that will crush her spirit if the employer is only going to pay her the same amount she can collect off unemployment? For one, it accelerates her laziness and refusal to be productive. There could be one argument that at least she's spending her days doing something productive, such as attempting to start up her own business, or helping out with a charity of her choice. She wasn't doing any of those things, but instead lying around the house watching television all day and surfing the Internet. There was no exercise or movement going on. Her days would finish up by meeting friends at the bars at night. This person fell into the toxic challenge of the Sloth.

This opens up larger discussions in the political arena about what is being done about how much people are getting paid at work. There has been an endless epidemic where employees make just enough money to live comfortably and stay afloat. Nearly half if not more of their check is going to living expenses. The cost of living, housing, and food continues to drive upwards, while the cost of paying employees stays relatively the same barely raising each year if at all. The work force doesn't make enough to set aside for retirement. This is going to create an even bigger problem when millions of people grow older and have little money in savings to survive on. No one is thinking deeply about that when you're a healthy thirty-four year old. This is another form of sloth, as well as greed coming from the employers. Lower rents, mortgages, clothing, and food costs if it will hurt businesses to raise employee wages.

Some have equated the sloth to be the person who cuts out of work early or calls in sick when they're not really ill. This goes back to the earlier point surrounding the break your back kind of work schedule that humankind created. Someone who is overworked and yet gets their job done is not a sloth when they choose to cut out of work early. Those who call in sick when they're not really ill is often attributed to being overworked without enough personal time. When you cut schedules to a reasonable amount where work gets done, then employees are more productive, happier, and less likely to call in when they have no reason to. While there are cases where people take advantage of the system, the average person is not doing that. They need to be cut some slack if they're an employee that regularly gets their job done.

Many reach a point of feeling spiritually dead throughout the course of their existence. Negative or challenging human life circumstances give birth to this experience. When you're in sloth mode, you are less likely to partake in activities that would ignite your spiritual essence. It's not uncommon to be guilty of any or all of the seven deadly sins and toxic challenges at one time or another. Don't beat yourself up if you fall into any of these categories, because I will be the first to raise my hand and announce I'm just as guilty. This is why I've included hints as to where I've fallen over the course of my life.

You're having a human experience and with that you will be tested from time to time. The testing is what your ego places on your back. The main reasons for illustrating the deadly sins is to be mindful of what will, or will not cut off your communication line with God, your Spirit team, and your higher self. This is to help you be aware of what could be contributing to any prolonged unhappiness in your life.

When you're deep in the throes of pride or lust, then you're driving through the fog without your headlights on. When you're in sloth mode, find ways to get focused, motivated, and productive again. Stay on track, remain organized, and have direction. Make those lists of what you need to get done, would like to accomplish, and then take action and get to it. Stay focused on your goals and continue moving forward in the right spirit!

Chapter Nine

ATHEISM AND ORGANIZED RELIGION: TWO EXTREME SIDES

*M*any in the world have turned against God because of the cruelty that some within organized religions have insisted upon. Judgment is not a word listed as a deadly sin, but it does fall into the category of pride. Everyone is on their own spiritual path and it is not anyone's job to shove their personal doctrine down the throats of another. The work I do and in my books has an open door policy. They're available for those who seek it out and are ready for it, but I don't run around the streets forcing it into someone's life. I don't hang on the corner with a sign telling people who walk by that they're going to Hell unless they read this. I talk about it if someone is deeply interested in the information. Some within the various organized religions do not observe this rule. They preach in judgment that promotes hate and destruction, which are traits not aligned with God. This has pushed people to turn away from all spiritual and religious related pursuits.

They hop over to the opposite extreme which is faithless. They cannot buy or believe that any decent God would prompt someone to criticize or harm someone else, nor can they believe that something they cannot see is real. This is where spirituality comes in.

Spirituality is a personal faith based belief system that doesn't demand that you harm, hate, or hurt others. Those who have true connections with God know that He is all about love. Do not be fooled otherwise since demons are the real wolves in sheep's clothing. God is aligned with the traits of love, joy, and peace.

Fundamentalists will criticize teachers of spirituality or those who are preaching about love to be false prophets, when they themselves are the true false prophets. False prophets teach and preach through the three H's: Hate, harm, hurt. This also means they believe Jesus Christ to be a false prophet since he was a Sage, profoundly psychic, and a spiritual preacher and believer.

The opposite extreme are atheists who are proud to be doubters because it's trendy at this time in history. Religions that are full of judgment and hate gave birth to atheism since no one is born religious or atheist. All souls are born spiritually connected. They feel the love, joy, and peace traits at a high level. Somewhere along the way through human tampering and the developmental process, those traits become greatly diminished.

Atheism and organized religion are beliefs that the child is taught and influenced to follow. Sometimes this happens indirectly where the child grows up in a household that either has no spiritual belief system, or it is surrounded by the opposite extreme, which is religious fanaticism.

Most become Christian or Muslim because they grew up in a household that is of that denomination. It influences the child to be part of it and convert to. This is done instead of allowing the child to find its own way and path. If this was not the case, then the person converts on their own at some point in their life for various reasons that feel right to them.

An atheist chooses not to believe in anything faith based because it's either fashionable among their peers, or they haven't had a profound enough connection with anything outside of themselves that prompts them to ask the bigger questions, or at least be open to the possibility that there is more. The media and popular culture is responsible for contributing to the rise in atheism. It emits distracting obsessions over triviality that kill off any spiritual essence the soul is born with.

The other reason for choosing atheism is because the person found organized religious dogma to be harmful. When you find religious dogma to be destructive, then it's best to find your own spiritual path that works for you, rather than denouncing all avenues of spiritual concepts just because you had to listen to hate filled words in a sermon, or because someone called you sinful your entire life.

Atheists believe that when you die, then it's the end. Everything goes black and you are without conscious. I've been listening to the words of spirit since I was a child. I was born connected with highly calibrated senses that pick up messages from beyond. Spirit has said things to me about others that there is no way I could know including stuff that ends up coming true. These stories are sprinkled throughout my work. If I hadn't had those experiences, then I probably would have been an atheist. I'm a fine tuned psychic sponge that it's impossible to shut it off. I'm picking up on everything to the point that it's too much.

The personal experiences I've had as a child and all through growing up prompted me to believe that the soul does not die. Nor does it experience a black out without consciousness. A deceased soul of a stranger I do not know is talking to me from somewhere telling me something the stranger is confirming. These little details sprinkled over the decades kept me a believer that this is not the end. We all go somewhere and are alive more than we've ever been after a human death. All souls have the capability and capacity to pick up on that information when they are connected and in a state of reception. All souls have access to messages and guidance when they are in tune.

When you are blocked and not connected, then

you pick up on nothing. This means the atheist is blocked, not connected, and heavily mired into the physical material world. When you're not absorbed into the physical world, then you will pick up on things that will begin to make you question, rather than denouncing all possibilities. Take a sabbatical to a nature preserve alone and spend some time away from all physical distractions and allow information to seep into your consciousness.

I've been a lifelong skeptic coupled with being a lifelong believer, since my mind works more on a practical analytical level. The skeptic part of me relies on some measure of proof that is convincing enough for me to believe. I've received those constant reminders all throughout my life, which makes me a lifelong believer, and yet I continue to test my Spirit team regardless. I could never personally choose atheism as a belief since I require that one constantly researches, questions, and tests the reasons for existence. Believing in nothing is no way for me to live, because then I would say, "What's the point of existing if this Hell on Earth is all that is?"

My mind has always been open enough to allow the answers to sift through me. Through my research and experiences I've discovered that many atheists are not as open minded as I've found those of varying faiths to be. Even though there are good and bad people of all faiths, gender, race, and sexual orientations. I've been attacked and criticized more by atheists than I have by those who are part of organized religions. I had grown up thinking it would be the opposite, and that atheists were the open minded tolerant cool ones, but through personal experience and research I've unfortunately found that to not be the case. There are exceptions as there are with anything, but this is a generalization meaning the majority.

Atheism for some is an excuse to behave badly towards other people and do as one pleases without consequence. I've had many atheists who do not know me attack with derogatory words. Those in organized religions are no different screaming the loudest using their faith as an excuse to harass others who do not follow the false words of past scripture. Both come from people operating from the darkness of one's ego attempting to shove their beliefs down someone's throat in a threatening and hostile way. I have never attempted to convert or convince anyone to follow what I believe and know. I merely teach and share the messages and make them readily available to those who are guided to it or genuinely ask about it.

One atheist had said that prayer doesn't work. He cited a piece about a couple who chose to use prayer in order to heal their premature infant instead of taking the child to the doctor. The child ended up dying because they didn't get the child medical attention. The couple was convicted of manslaughter. This is an example of extremists from both sides of the fence.

It's dangerous to immediately come to the not thought out conclusion that prayer doesn't work, when in fact prayer or positive thoughts have assisted millions around the world for centuries and continue to do so. I've witnessed miraculous intervention and assistance only after I submitted a prayer and asked for help. When I did not do that, then the pain or whatever I was experiencing continued without letting up.

The other extreme side was that the religious couple prayed instead of taking their child to the doctor. Had the religious couple been in tune without blocks, then they would've received the guidance urging them to bring the child to receive medical attention by a professional. This is a great example of how easily influenced both sides are and immediately come to an abrupt conclusion because of what they were trained to do instead of diving deeper. Become a lifelong student testing the various theories out for yourself instead of coming to the final conclusion because someone else said so.

Both atheism and organized religions will gradually diminish over time. There have been newer generations of souls being born who are highly connected and open minded than those who exist at this time in history. It has gradually being heading in that direction. Many have been moving away from organized religion in larger numbers. This will have a domino effect of not influencing someone to flip to the other extreme side of no belief. This gives rise to those who follow an open minded faith of loving and accepting all with compassion. This is already being seen in younger generations who are not religious, but they are not atheist either. They are being drawn into some form of spirituality. They are growing up less blocked with a fine tuned divine detector. They know that the state of humanity is in a dangerous place and that life is not all about popular culture, social media, and knocking people down to get what you want.

The misconception many have is that God is sitting up on a throne above the clouds kicking back and watching all of Earth's atrocities and not doing a thing. God is in every space that exists. There is no running from Him. He's in every cell, atom, and centimeter of matter that is around. There is no escape or running from Him. He is in the terrorists, the non believers, as well as you and I. There are pieces of Him in every living soul. It may be hard to believe that God is in the terrorists, but He is in there somewhere. They have just been unable to access Him. If they ever wake up to reality, then they might be able to get a glimpse of Him before their life run is over.

God is the good parts of one's soul. When you exude love, joy, and peace, then you are displaying pieces of God. Look up the words joy and what do you get? Satisfaction, bliss, delight, wonder, rejoicing, cheer, humor. When you look up love, you get devotion, passion, tenderness, friendship, affection, cherishing, enjoyment. With peace you get harmony, unity, calm, quiet, tranquility. All of these adjectives are states of being that one's true soul desires and thrives for.

There are millions of souls on the other side working tirelessly to wake the planet up through individual human souls. These are the people who suddenly wake up at some point in their life to realize there is more to this Earthly physical world nonsense than hate, negativity, and violence. There are also souls in a human body doing what they can as well. Since most don't listen to their Spirit team, these souls have incarnated on Earth to contribute their part. Every little bit of contributions to humanity helps.

You lose faith when you witness violence or harm done to others or even on yourself. One can become confused wondering why if there is Divine intelligence, God or a creator, then why does this force not intervene automatically to help. The laws of God and the Universe include that no spirit being, Archangel, Angel, Ascended Master, Saint, Departed Loved One, Realm Spirit - you name it - no spirit being can intervene in any other spirit being's life without permission from that soul. It is the free will law. It doesn't matter how horrid any measure of violence is acted out at the hands of humankind. They cannot intervene as it is impossible. All are restricted from that including God Himself. If He was to intervene and stop these heinous acts, then the Earth wouldn't exist since human souls have been committing these wrathful vengeful crimes since the dawn of man. He would be slapping quite a bit of souls from that enraged place and the soul wouldn't learn anything.

If He came in and stopped it, then no one would be here since all souls exude a deadly sin at one point or another. All souls would be killed and burned off. Earth is the bottom of the barrel and the Hell dimension so to speak. It doesn't get any lower than that. Earth is Hell because the darkness of ego has made it a place that is the opposite of paradise. It is not God's job to stop that from happening. It doesn't matter how barbaric human souls are behaving. That's not His fault or His problem that no one can control their ego. Learn to control your ego and find the space of love, joy, and peace in order to move to higher destinies.

You are your own authority so avoid putting anyone on a pedestal. Idolatry is an extreme worship of anything or anyone. This includes celebrities you bow down to. They are people who are flawed just as any other human soul, but are eerily treated like royalty.

When harm is done to another, ones ego wants God to do something about the violence. It is not His job to clean up someone else's mess. If a parent did everything for their child, then the child wouldn't learn anything and would expect everything to be taken care of on a whim. If you want something to be done, then do it. Show and teach compassion and love to the world since this is lacking. If this existed and people weren't blinded by the truth, then there would be peace on Earth.

Major catastrophes are what shakes the world up from slumber. Love is forgotten until there is a tragedy. Catastrophes that are not nature related come about due to free will choice. It is a statement that wakes the world up in the process without the intention of doing that. When one gets too comfortable, they get sloppy, stop paying attention, and neglect to live in the space of love.

There is no true soul death. The physical body dies on Earth, but the soul is everlasting and continues on with no pain. Pain is connected to the physical body in the Earthly plane. Human ego sees the pain and suffering in others who have lost loved ones, but that is the cycle of human life.

Human souls become attached to one another. It hurts and grows painful when someone you love is taken away from you abruptly without warning. This is whether in Earthly death or in an ending by leaving your life. They will all see each other again when the individual life run has completed. The human ego doubts this and is saddened believing they are gone for good. Heaven already knows where you go when your life run has completed. The human mind is instinctual and it develops attachments to people and things. It grows upset when these things are taken away. All of this is temporary once your purpose is fulfilled and you exit your body. Your perspective is broader and more profound back home on the other side.

Chapter Ten

CONNECTING WITH YOUR SPIRIT TEAM

You are a conscious, thinking, feeling, soul light born out of love and having a physical human experience. At the beginning of your Earthly life, you were born profoundly psychic and in tune to all that is around you. You basked in the traits of love, joy, and peace full time. This is your true soul's essence. Whenever you stray outside of that you are no longer aligned with God or higher level Spirit beings in Heaven. Instead, your ego has risen and taken over your soul's true essence.

You were born with an ego that expands as it enters the Earth's atmosphere. This ego causes you to struggle and have conflicts as it attempts to take over you and dominate your actions, thoughts, and feelings. When your ego runs recklessly it grows and expands into darkness. The dark ego is what prompts you to wrestle with challenges in this lifetime. These challenges were called *sin* during ancient times, even though some circles continue to keep the word alive. It's used in a big way in this book, but in the modern day world the word is best understood as *challenges*. The sins committed can delay you on your path and wreak havoc on your soul's innate system. This innate system is the higher self part of you that governs your life through a broader perspective.

The seven deadly sins were created in order to assist human souls in making sounder choices. As time progressed, these sins were soon viewed as extreme depending on who was executing them. This eventually tainted the deadly sins into something evil. They were disregarded and not taken seriously except in smaller religious based circles. Although the seven deadly sins have underlying religious based tones, they are challenges that all human souls wrestle with to one degree or another regardless of religion.

Having an understanding of the core seven deadly sins is not for anyone's benefit, but your own. When you're deeply absorbed in these toxic challenges, then it causes an array of issues and complications on your life path. These sins or challenges prevent the positive flow of energy and abundance in your life. They also play a hand at creating a block that stops up the communication line with your team on the Other Side.

After reading through the seven core deadly

sins, you likely noticed where you had partaken in them in some form or another. You also might have noticed how this prevented something positive from coming about in your life as a result. As you read the potential meanings and descriptions, you discovered there are varying levels of each sin committed. This means sometimes you naively partake in one level of one of the sins, but it doesn't create as huge of a block as it might when you abuse another on a different level.

You think super highly of yourself to the point where you've moved into Pride sin territory. The light side of the Pride challenge is self-worth and self-confidence. It's harmless for the most part as opposed to committing the deadly sin of wrath where you are immersed in vengeance against someone because they live a different life with diverse values than you do. The latter causes the bigger blocks between yourself and what you desire. This is also between yourself and the communication line with God, as well as yourself and your higher self's path.

As you grew from infant into childhood, the peers, community, and society around you played a major hand at your developmental process. They implemented belief systems and values that although might have been brought to you without malice, they ultimately erected blocks in your path and dimmed the communication line with Heaven. As a result, you might have questioned the existence of anything outside of yourself because you stopped picking up any signs of your Spirit teams guidance and messages.

You can tell if this is the case or not by going back into time and remembering how you were raised and what those around you were like. How much of your values and ways of living today are similar to what your caregivers and peers were like growing up? If they are on par and similar, then this is an example of how you were heavily influenced by those around you. If you're a Christian, Buddhist, or Muslim, and so we're most of those around you growing up, then this is another sign of being influenced by your surroundings. You adopted the way of life you were taught by those in your vicinity. This doesn't necessarily mean it's a bad thing. You're examining how your values and beliefs today have indeed been heavily influenced by those around you. This continues on into adulthood as you adopt new values and beliefs that your social circles follow.

If you're in love with a potential political ruler or candidate, odds are that your peers have the same love. If it's not a candidate, then it's a political party. Some will stand firm on their personal moral rule that they cannot be friends with anyone who does not share their beliefs or values. While they might deny this and emphatically ensure they love all, this turns out not to be the case when an isolated circumstance pushes them to reconsider their tolerance level. This is especially the case where religion and politics are concerned. Two topics that should never be discussed at a dinner gathering or at work. Those with differing opinions cannot be convinced to see it your way and vice versa.

You can be friends with those who have diverse political or religious beliefs from yourself, and still be able to remain close because you have other elements outside of that which bring you together. You naturally don't get into conversations on topics where you know it is opposing of one another. And when you do discuss it, you are respectful of one another's beliefs.

Someone who came into this lifetime as a homosexual can be friends with someone who grew up Christian in this lifetime. This is as long as the Christian has no issues with their friend who is gay and vice versa. It would be debatable on how close of a friend two people are if a big part of them is rejected by their friend.

Christians receive a bad rap because the media has focused heavily on the ones who claim that being homosexual is a sin. The real sin are those absolved in the seven deadly sins, which include Pride (judgment) and Wrath (hate). Heaven has taught me over the years that there is nothing sinful about two souls coming together in love, regardless of their human physical gender. Human souls have free will choice to believe what they want to believe, even if it's not based in reality.

There are a great many wonderful loving Christians who love all souls without condition as long as the soul is not hurting anyone. You rarely hear about them because the media finds anything connected to goodness to be too boring for a story or worth talking about.

The world witnesses someone preaching hate,

but then you investigate how that person was raised only to discover that this persons caregivers and surroundings were like that as well. There are cases where someone's values are erroneously distinctive. You were raised in a positively joyful home with suitable values, but you dart off in the opposite direction into a life of hate or negativity. Every human soul being is a complex character with a mixture of attributes that come in from various sources. The best parts of a human soul are the ones that are a part of God. The worst parts are where the ego has been led astray.

There are many clair *(clear)* channels within every soul, but there are four primary clairs. They are Clairvoyance *(clear seeing)*, Clairsentience *(clear feeling)*, Clairaudience *(clear hearing)* and Claircognizance *(clear knowing)*. These clairs are the channel frequencies in which you communicate with God or any spirit soul being in Heaven.

You were intended to have a strong connection and communication line with Heaven. This gift is not a gift at all as it's part of who you are. It is already built into the core part of your soul.

Your team consists of one Spirit Guide and one Guardian Angel. Every soul on Earth has this without exception. Your core duo team is with you from the day of your human birth up until your human death. They are one of the two that greets you as you enter the gates of Heaven. They are your team who works with you guiding you away from harm and down the path that benefits your higher self. In a sense, they do their best to help you along your life's path. This can be to assist you in picking out a school or trade course aligned with your purpose, or to finding a job, an apartment, or potential love interest that will be beneficial for you.

One of the other reasons your guardians are with you is in order to assist you in accomplishing the varying purposes you agreed upon prior to entering an Earthly life. If you are someone who has a strong connection with the other side, you pray to God regularly, you're going through tough human life experiences, or have a purpose that is beneficial to the betterment of humanity and this planet, then you likely have more than one guide or angel outside of your primary heavenly teammate duo. Even though your team is with you, often many are unaware of their presence. Your team and any soul being in Heaven cannot intervene or assist you in your life without your expressed permission. This is due to that free will law previously mentioned. The law says you will need to request your Spirit team's assistance or guidance. This is also why so many people are led astray down inappropriate or harmful roads. They are either not asking for their team to work with them daily, or they do not believe that there is such a thing.

For the most part, your Spirit team will assist a human soul by giving them nudges to head in a direction that will positively benefit them. They will communicate with that soul through their senses and hope the human soul is paying attention.

127

Their job is to help you make sounder choices, but as for anything outside of that, they need your permission. You can give them permission in prayer, affirmations, with your thoughts, out loud, or in writing. You can even write them an email and send it to yourself. You call to them and say something like, "I give you permission to intervene with..." It doesn't matter how you say it, just as long as you let them know.

Your soul is built with innate crystal clear senses for a reason. This is to make your life as comfortable as possible even when you're faced with challenges. The challenges are not as bad as they would be without your strong connection with Heaven. They help you make smarter choices by guiding you.

Everyone is born with all clair channels, but typically one or two of the channels are stronger than the others. If you feel that you do not have any clair channels, then that means there are blocks that have closed it up, because everyone has these clairs. No one is more special than anyone else where psychic abilities are concerned. Everyone has varying ways in which they communicate and pick up on Divine assistance.

Someone might have a stronger Clairaudience channel where they hear the voice of spirit, while another person might have a strong sense of knowing the answers. Others feel the guidance coming into them, and then you have the Clairvoyants who receive messages through visual cues. The clairs are always there and accessible to you. They can be opened up when you make healthy positive life changes. When you govern your life through negativity, then this closes the clair channels up. This means that your moods, thoughts, and feelings affect the extra sensory part of you.

When you regularly fall down the path of abusing any of the deadly sins, then you will find your clair channels dim to the point that you're unaware of these senses being present at all. Those who run around making negative based comments vocally, or online, have zero connection with anything outside of themselves at that moment. If they do this regularly, then they are indefinitely disconnected from God. A soulless being is someone who does this on a frequent basis. This type of *egoic* criticism does nothing to help anyone. It doesn't help anyone reading those comments and absorbing the energy surrounding those words. They have no connection to anything outside of the physical. Those connected with Heaven operate from a higher space than those who are bathed in hate and negativity. This includes spiritually based people, since no one of any group is exempt from hanging out in the areas of negativity, including myself. This is part of the challenges of the physical human life to overcome.

Your Spirit team is made up of one Spirit Guide and one Guardian Angel. They are present during your Earthly birth and remain with you all throughout your life until you pass on. They are one of the many that greet you when you cross over back home. You might have more than one guide and angel if you are someone who works with Heaven more than others do, or if you have a big goal you're working on that requires additional spiritual support.

The purpose of your Spirit team is to assist you in guiding you along your life path. They do this by communicating with you through one or multiple clairs with information, messages, and guidance that can assist you in a positive way. This includes working with you to guide you towards your desires pending those needs are aligned with your higher self. This means they'll help you find the right work in the area of your passionate interest, but may not help you win the lottery, since lottery numbers are generated through free will and cannot be accurately predicted. Being handed a huge monetary financial gain without working for it usually doesn't help one's soul growth. It does not benefit the person's higher self. Heaven grants blessings that will assist in the growth of that person. There are a number of cases where someone poor won a huge lump sum in the lottery and somehow managed to lose all of it not long after that. They did not have to work for it, so therefore had no idea how to budget efficiently and disburse the money in a way that brings balance to that individual's life.

Spiritual books have increased in great numbers from the 20th Century and beyond. Before that time, spiritualists were considered witches and burned at the stake. They were seen as a threat or connected to the Devil, rather than God. Times have changed drastically where human souls who are highly connected have been incarnated like mad. Others began to have an understanding of what the spiritualist was talking about as they were having these experiences too. This is because all souls have this connection to God. The Dark Ages have been gradually fading ever so slightly away to make room for the true light.

Today there are numerous books written through the author's divine guidance in order to assist humanity in getting into soul shape. The material is intended to help in fine tuning your soul, mind, and body. This is in order to elevate your life into a happier state, as well as to help you pay attention to what's outside of the physical world. If everyone listened to God, Heaven, and their Spirit team full time, then Earthly life would be bliss for all.

Not everyone enjoys the same author, even if all author's talk about similar content. The one reason there are so many teachers is because some readers will respond to one teacher and not another, while other readers will respond strongly to one that you do not. The point is that there are more people being reached through all of the teachers that incarnated on the planet at any particular time.

You create your circumstances through your intention. Avoid falling into a victim mentality where you blame everything that goes wrong in your life on other people. Or that you did something to make it happen and must have done something bad in another life to deserve it. No one deserves bad things to happen to them, but you have the gift of standing in your power and taking control of your life. You don't have to do it alone when you have God on your side.

When you pay attention to your Spirit team, then you are able to pick up on when they are guiding you away from harm, or when they guide you towards helpful circumstances. A common theme of the ego is living in denial of the truth. You deny the messages because it's not what you want to hear. It is unpleasing to the human ego. Sometimes the messages intended to assist are guiding someone to do something they're against. This can be a circumstance where you're consistently guided to let go of the possibility of a love relationship with someone you desire. Your Spirit team can see how it will end up ahead and it will not end happily in your favor. Or they see the Soul Mate relationship partner you're contracted to connect with coming in soon. Being with the wrong person may delay the connection from happening.

How many times have you received a nudge to go down one road, but instead you went down another? The result was that something negative or challenging popped up in your life. You later say, "I knew I shouldn't have gone down that road. I sensed something was up, but I ignored that feeling." This is a clue as to how your Spirit team is working with you.

The ways people connect with Heaven are vast and varying from one person to the next. Many of my books include the different ways that can assist someone in being a stronger conduit. This includes a lifestyle and attitude perception change that needs to be adopted. This is from the way you think and feel, to what you ingest into your physical body.

When you shift direction and embark on a beautiful personal spiritual journey, then you will find wonderful and amazing new circumstances rise up. Even if this is a feeling and state of mind. This state of mind is where true bliss resides. There is no end date, time limit, or rush to reach the destination you're hoping to achieve. Take your time with it and follow your gut instincts on what action steps to take.

Some try so hard to make a connection with God not realizing that it's the trying so hard part that pushes the connection away. Most of the time the connection with Heaven happens when you're not trying so hard. When you let go of the control, then it comes. This is what that phrase, "Let go and Let God", means. Learn to know yourself better than anybody. Trust your initial gut reaction to hunches that hit you. When you second guess the message you believe you're picking up on, then you move further away from the message or guidance you originally got. If you're receiving a strong hunch that continuously comes to you, then make note of that. The hunch will be something positive that does no harm to anyone, including yourself.

Afterword

I've talked about the transition into the next plane briefly in my book, *Divine Messages for Humanity*. I've also revealed tidbits here and there in my other books sporadically. I've mentioned this tunnel of light before, which at this point many are already aware of. However, it's not actually a tunnel of light and nor is it a staircase as some artwork suggests. The artwork depiction of a stairway to Heaven is a metaphor.

Human beings are etheric souls inhabiting a physical body in order to reside in this physical plane for what is called a human lifetime. When you pass on and separate from this body, there is an etheric substance that is attached to the etheric spirit part of you that pulls out of it and stretches at a slight angle.

This begins in darkness at the floor and gradually grows lighter and brighter as you move along with it. Eventually by the time you reach the other side, the light becomes so bright it's overwhelming. You know that you are no longer on the Earth plane. This slight angle *etheric* road as I'll call it makes sense considering that the next spirit dimension is about three feet above us and runs parallel along with this dimension.

The first presence you're greeted by begins with one person. It's typically someone who is super familiar to you. It might even be a deity that you are super close with. Eventually the *others* appear not long after you have your initial introduction. This is to make the transition as calmly as possible.

This tunnel source grows brighter as you cross over back home, but the irony is it's reversed in a sense as you enter an Earthly life. There is a similar transition into your human life that begins less comfortably. It's a discombobulating feeling as your soul becomes entrapped in this new physical casing. You feel the weight and heaviness being pressed upon you that it's almost a strangulation. This is partially why most babies are crying when they are born. It's the jarring adjustment into learning to function in this physical body with organs that were obsolete as a soul. You're now having to learn to breathe through the human lungs.

~

I am in Heaven staring back at myself, except I look better than the human physical me radiating light all around my soul. It is a light so bright that it almost looks like there are wings at the top of my shoulders, but it's hard to tell because it's too bright. I look up ahead and one of my friends moves in front of me confused and disoriented, then they immediately flood with tears. They know who I am and remember me from Earth. I smile slightly and move both my hands to the sides and say, "Welcome home."

When my hands fly to the side everything behind me is immediately filled in with an astronomical and indescribable paradise of color. It's filling in like a paint by number set. I focus on my friend who is surrounded by angels moving in close. I fly my hands forward towards him and then outwards to the sides causing black tar to fly out of his soul. I say calmly, "Getting rid of some of this remaining Earth gunk. You don't need it anymore. Your home now." I smile, "And you've had a wild ride." Soon other relatives of my friend are appearing behind me out of nowhere. They're walking out of the paradise like moving through a doorway from one dimension to another. They approach him to take over. This is the beginning of his souls journey in Heaven.

†

Available in paperback and E-book
by Kevin Hunter,
"Ignite Your Inner Life Force"

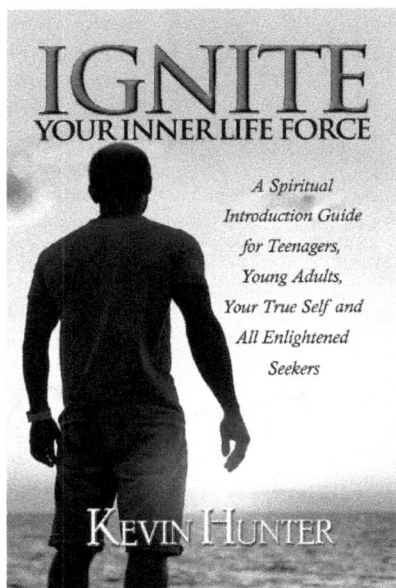

Ignite Your Inner Life Force is an introduction guide for teens, young adults, and anyone seeking answers, messages, and guidance and surrounding spiritual empowerment. This is from understanding what Heaven, the soul, and spiritual beings are to knowing when you are connecting with your Spirit team of Guides and Angels.

Some of the topics covered are communicating with Heaven, working with your Spirit team, what your higher self is, your life purpose and soul contract, what the ego is, love and relationships, your vibration energy, shifting your consciousness and thinking for yourself even when you stand alone. This is an in-depth primer manual offering you foundation as you find a higher purpose navigating through your personal journey in today's modern day practical world.

Available in paperback and E-book
by Kevin Hunter,
"Awaken Your Creative Spirit"

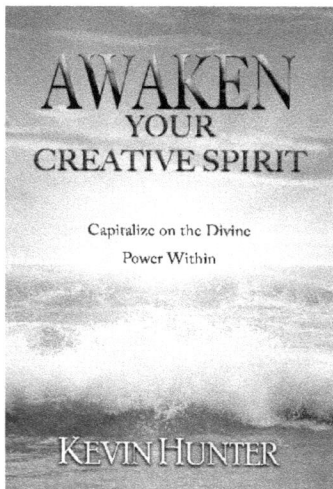

Your creative spirit is present when you experience positive energy flowing through you. This energy is ignited when you make a direct connection with God. This vibration state is where you have access to the true you, which is your higher self. Your higher self rules when you work to strip, reduce, or dissolve any negative tampering influenced by a domination of your physical surroundings.

Your creative spirit is more than being artistic and getting involved in creativity pursuits, although this is a good part of it. When your creative spirit is activated by a high vibration state of being, then this is the space you create from. You can apply this to your dealings in life, your creative and artistic pursuits, and to having a greater communication line with your Spirit team on the Other Side.

Your creative spirit brings your soul into a high vibration state of being because coming from a place of creativity raises your vibration. This is the place where you create and manifest your visions at higher levels while moving you into the joy of your life. It is thinking like a kid, unleashing your inner artist, and realizing your soul's potential. When you claim your celestial power with the assistance of your heavenly helpers by your side on your Earthly life, then this assists in capitalizing the true divine power within you.

Awaken Your Creative Spirit is an overview of what it means to have access to Divine assistance and how that plays a part in arousing the muse within you in order to bring your state of mind into a happier space.

138

Available in paperback and E-book
by Kevin Hunter,
"Realm of the Wise One"

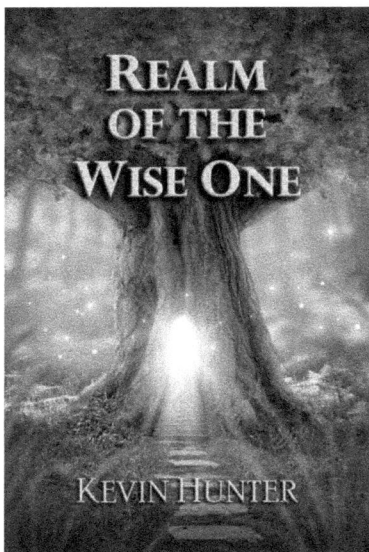

In the Spirit Worlds and the dimensions that exist, reside numerous kingdoms that house a plethora of Spirits that inhabit various forms. One of these tribes is called the Wise Ones, a darker breed in the spirit realm who often chooses to incarnate into a human body one lifetime after another for important purposes.

The *Realm of the Wise One* takes you on a magical journey to the spirit world where the Wise Ones dwell. This is followed with in-depth and detailed information on how to recognize a human soul who has incarnated from the Wise One Realm.

Author, Kevin Hunter, is a Wise One who uses the knowledge passed onto him by his Spirit team of Guides and Angels to relay the wisdom surrounding all things Wise One. He discusses the traits, purposes, gifts, roles, and personalities among other things that make up someone who is a Wise One.

Wise Ones have come in the guises of teachers, shaman, leaders, hunters, mediums, entertainers and others. *Realm of the Wise One* is an informational guide devoted to the tribe of the Wise Ones, both in human form and on the other side.

Available in paperback
and E-book
by Kevin Hunter,

"Reaching for the Warrior
Within"

Reaching for the Warrior Within is the author's personal story recounting a volatile childhood. This led him to a path of addictions, anxiety and overindulgence in alcohol, drugs, cigarettes and destructive relationships. As a survival mechanism, he split into many different "selves". He credits turning his life around, not by therapy, but by simultaneously paying attention to the messages he has been receiving from his Spirit team in Heaven since birth.

Kevin Hunter gains strength, healing and direction with the help of his own team of guides and angels. Living vicariously through this inspiring story will enable you to distinguish when you have been assisted on your own life path. *Reaching for the Warrior Within* attests that anyone can change if they pay attention to their own inner guidance system and take action. This can be from being a victim of child abuse, or a drug and alcohol user, to going after the jobs and relationships you want. This powerful story is for those seeking motivation to change, alter and empower their life one day at a time.

Available in paperback and E-book
by Kevin Hunter,

"WARRIOR OF LIGHT
Messages from my Guides and Angels"

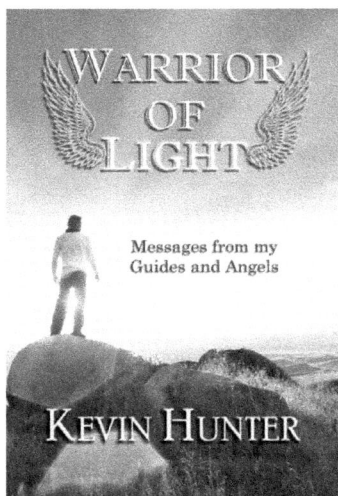

There are legions of angels, spirit guides, and departed loved ones in heaven that watch and guide you on your journey here on Earth. They are around to make your life easier and less stressful. Do you pay attention to the nudges, guidance, and messages given to you? There are many who live lives full of negativity and stress while trying to make ends meet. This can shake your faith as it leads you down paths of addictions, unhealthy life choices, and negative relationship connections. Learn how you can recognize the guidance of your own Spirit team of guides and angels around you.

Author, Kevin Hunter, relays heavenly guided messages about getting humanity, the world, and yourself into shape. He delivers the guidance passed onto him by his own Spirit team on how to fine tune your body, soul and raise your vibration. Doing this can help you gain hope and faith in your own life in order to start attracting in more abundance.

Available in paperback and E-book
by Kevin Hunter,

Empowering Spirit Wisdom
A Warrior of Light's Guide on Love, Career and the Spirit World"

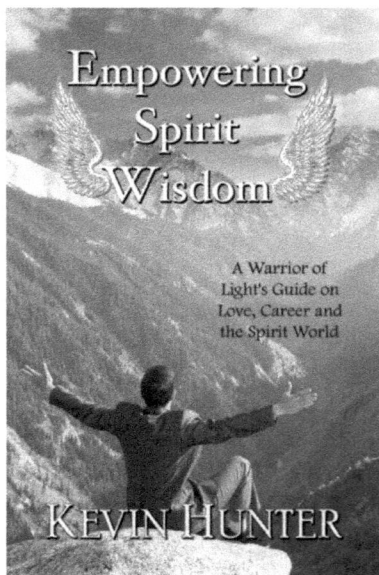

Kevin Hunter relays heavenly, guided messages for everyday life concerns with his book, *Empowering Spirit Wisdom.* Some of the topics covered are your soul, spirit and the power of the light, laws of attraction, finding meaningful work, transforming your professional and personal life, navigating through the various stages of dating and love relationships, as well as other practical affirmations and messages from the Archangels. Kevin Hunter passes on the sensible wisdom given to him by his own Spirit team in this inspirational book.

"Darkness of Ego"

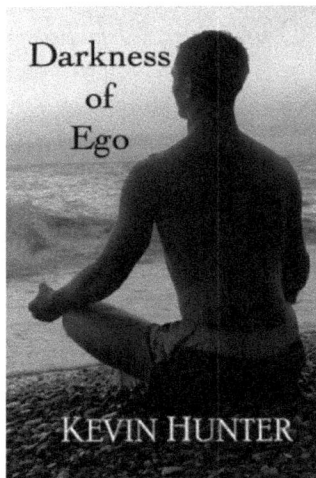

The biggest cause of turmoil and conflict in one's life is executed by the human ego. All souls have an ego. The most unruly and destructive ego exists within every human soul. When the soul enters into a physical human body, the ego immediately compresses and then swells up. It is the higher self's goal to ensure that it remains in check while living an Earthly life.

The ego is what tests each soul along its journey. It is how one learns right from wrong. The experiences and challenges that the soul has while living in this Earthly life school contribute to the soul's growth. When a soul learns lessons, it is intended and expected to grow and enhance from the experience. Yet, there are a great many souls who do not learn lessons and remain in the same spot. The ill of the bunch wreaks all kinds of havoc, destruction, judgment and heart ache in its wake.

In *Darkness of Ego*, author Kevin Hunter infuses some of the guidance, messages, and wisdom he's received from his Spirit team surrounding all things ego related. The ego is one of the most damaging culprits in human life. Therefore it is essential to understand the nature of the beast in order to navigate gracefully out of it when it spins out of control. Some of the topics covered in *Darkness of Ego* are humanity's destruction, mass hysteria, karmic debt, and the power of the mind, heaven's gate, the ego's war on love and relationships, and much more.

The *Warrior of Light* series of mini-pocket books are available in paperback and E-book by Kevin Hunter called, *Spirit Guides and Angels, Soul Mates and Twin Flames, Divine Messages for Humanity, Raising Your Vibration, Connecting with the Archangels*

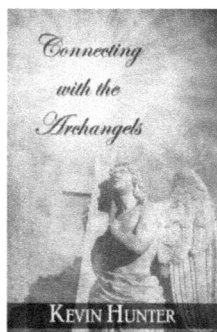

About KEVIN HUNTER

Kevin Hunter is an author, love expert and channeler. His books tackle a variety of genres and tend to have a strong male protagonist. The messages and themes he weaves in his work surround Spirit's own communications of love and respect which he channels and infuses into his writing and stories.

His books include the Warrior of Light series of books, *Warrior of Light, Empowering Spirit Wisdom, Realm of the Wise One, Reaching for the Warrior Within, Darkness of Ego, Ignite Your Inner Life Force, Awaken Your Creative Spirit,* and *The Seven Deadly Sins.* He is also the author of the horror, drama, *Paint the Silence,* and the modern day erotic love story, *Jagger's Revolution.*

Before writing books and stories, Kevin started out in the entertainment business in 1996 becoming actress Michelle Pfeiffer's personal development dude for her boutique production company, Via Rosa Productions. She dissolved her company after several years and he made a move into coordinating film productions for the big studios on such films as *One Fine Day, A Thousand Acres, The Deep End of the Ocean, Crazy in Alabama, Original Sin, The Perfect Storm, Harry Potter & the Sorcerer's Stone, Dr. Dolittle 2* and *Carolina.* He considers himself a love addict and beach bum born and raised in Los Angeles, California.

Visit www.kevin-hunter.com